Can You See It?

CAN YOU SEE IT?

**He has set eternity in our hearts,
yet we cannot fathom
the work He has done**

GRAEME SCHULTZ

Gobsmacked Publishing

All Scripture quotations, unless otherwise indicated, are taken from the Holy Bible, New International Version®, NIV®. Copyright ©1973, 1978, 1984, 2011 by Biblica, Inc.™ Used by permission of Zondervan. All rights reserved worldwide. www.zondervan.com The "NIV" and "New International Version" are trademarks registered in the United States Patent and Trademark Office by Biblica, Inc.™

Copyright © 2019 by Graeme Schultz

First published January 2019

All rights reserved. No part of this publication may be reproduced, distributed or transmitted in any form or by any means, including photocopying, recording, or other electronic or mechanical methods, without the prior written permission of the publisher, except in the case of brief quotations embodied in critical reviews and certain other non-commercial uses permitted by copyright law. For permission requests, write to the publisher, addressed "Permissions Coordinator," at the address below.

Graeme Schultz/Gobsmacked Publishing

19 Trotters Lane
Cudgee, Victoria, Australia, 3265

Email: graeme@design2build.net.au

www.gobsmackedpublishing.com.au

Cataloguing-in-Publication Data:

Author: Schultz, Graeme

Email: graeme@design2build.net.au

Title: Can You See It?

Subjects: Devotional

Can You See It?

Graeme Schultz

ISBN 978-0-6484690-0-1 (paperback)

ISBN 978-0-6484690-1-8 (ebook)

Typeset by bookbound.com.au

Contents

Introduction		vii
Chapter 1	Truman	1
Chapter 2	The Beginning	5
Chapter 3	The Dome	8
Chapter 4	The System Under The Dome	12
Chapter 5	Spiritual Sight	17
Chapter 6	Self-Conscious	19
Chapter 7	Identity	22
Chapter 8	The Spirit	24
Chapter 9	The Mind Of Adam	27
Chapter 10	God's Logic	30
Chapter 11	A Scaled-Down God	33
Chapter 12	Who Am I?	36
Chapter 13	The Divine Nature	39
Chapter 14	The Eyes Of The Heart	41
Chapter 15	God's View Of Things	44
Chapter 16	The Cost	47
Chapter 17	The God Kind Of Love	50
Chapter 18	The Better Way	53
Chapter 19	The Natural Realm	56
Chapter 20	The Kingdom Of God	60

Chapter 21	The Sin Problem	63
Chapter 22	Faith	65
Chapter 23	Beyond Theology	68
Chapter 24	Empty	72
Chapter 25	My Movie	74
Chapter 26	In The Father	78
Chapter 27	The New Me	81
Chapter 28	Spirit And Truth	85
Chapter 29	Life In The Spirit	88

Introduction

Have you ever wondered what's on the other side? Most of us are so preoccupied with life in the here and now that we hardly stop to think about what eternity is actually like. It is, after all, a long way off for most of us—so we think we can give it some thought when it looms a little larger.

However, the Bible speaks of eternity as "present tense," i.e. we are in it now. John 5:24 tells us that we have eternal life as soon as we believe in Jesus. So it begs the question, "If eternity is real and present, why can't we see it? What is stopping us from perceiving its reality?"

It's an important question because our identity is intrinsically linked to our environment, and so we need to be people who actually live in the environment of the kingdom Jesus restored to us. To do this, we must examine the reality of the realm of God and decide if we really are in it.

CHAPTER 1

Truman

I remember watching the movie "The Truman Show" in which the star, Truman Burbank (played by Jim Carey), lives out his life in an entirely fabricated world. After watching the movie, I wondered if that was actually possible—to live life in a world that is not what it seems.

Every day Truman would go about his life in the seaside town of Seahaven Island; he would go to work, meet his friends and generally live out his life in a make-believe environment that was fake in every way: the town was a gigantic movie set complete with an artificial sky dome, his friends were paid actors, and thousands of hidden cameras captured his every move. Truman's daily interactions were all scripted—he just didn't know it. He was stuck in a figment of the movie director's imagination…and he had no idea.

The movie's creator and director, Christof, created the set, controlled Truman by telling him he couldn't leave the island due to his fear of water, and responded to Truman's every move by directing the actors and cameras.

Every day millions of viewers watched this reality TV program. Truman's make-believe life was a national fascination, which would ultimately culminate in a movement to set him free from his fake existence.

But the whole thing was based on a lie.
Truman couldn't see the bigger picture of his life.

Truman knew something wasn't right; some things just didn't seem to add up, and after a few false starts, he overcame his fear of water, sailed his little boat through a storm and bumped into the edge of the movie set. His boat punctured the artificial dome, and he found an exit door—his doorway into the real world.

This movie set was Truman's entire world; it was all he had ever known. All his history and memories were contained in Seahaven Island. He had no reason to believe that a bigger world even existed—yet, deep inside, he knew one did. Some inner instinct drove him on even though he had no tangible idea of what lay on the outside.

The physical evidence found in Seahaven Island didn't present Truman with an alternative reality, in fact the physical evidence agreed with his single-dimensioned existence; it was his heart that drove him on to seek more—not his head.

However, Truman still had to overcome his fears; he still had to learn to listen to his heart, and he still had to "risk it all" to embrace his bigger life. In the end, Truman's true identity in the real world was held back by just one thing—Truman. He knew deep down there was more to life than his safe little make-believe world; he just had to decide which world he would allow to contain him.

Truman was like an unpaid actor performing for the viewing audience. He didn't know that everything he said and did was providing entertainment for millions; he was merely a pawn who unwittingly responded to the script that was subtly woven around him by Christof.

> **His life was the product of someone else's agenda.**

The fact of the matter is that, without Truman's conscious knowledge, he was actually living in two worlds at the same time. His little movie-set world of Seahaven Island was contained within the much bigger world at large, and Truman lived in both simultaneously—one consciously, and the other without any awareness. Truman didn't actually need to travel to an entirely different location to connect with the real world; all he needed to do was venture beyond the fake reality of the lesser one. The big wide world was right there, waiting for him to step into it.

In many respects, the only thing that stopped Truman from living in these two worlds seamlessly and in perfect harmony was the artificial dome between them. If there had been no dome, then he could have remained in Seahaven enjoying the man-made environment for what it was while knowing that his real identity was established in a much bigger reality.

This book is primarily about identity and reality. Truman had an identity crisis because he was shaped by a false reality. And we also will struggle to discover who we really are if we embrace the false reality reported to us by life on planet earth…*we are so much more than we seem.*

I enjoyed the movie for its entertainment value, and I am also thankful for the poignant illustration it provides about the Christian life. I will refer back to "The Truman Show" as we progress through this book. In fact, I would recommend a short detour to view the movie if you are so inclined; it might help you to get a better handle on the subject matter as we go along.

The Bible also talks about two worlds; they are sometimes referred to as realms or kingdoms.

As I watched "The Truman Show," I was exposed to two dramas unfolding in two separate worlds. I could see Truman's life lived out in the smaller world, and I could see the movie's TV audience interacting in their own way in the larger world. It was easy to make the distinction between these two worlds as I watched the movie; they were both clearly on display, and they were both supported by their respective physical context.

The two worlds referred to in the Bible are not as easily distinguished. The natural realm has the environmental makeup with which we are familiar—people, trees, houses and so on. These are the markers of our day-to-day existence in our physical world.

The spiritual realm is less familiar. It doesn't contain any material item, yet it is the bigger and more real environment by far.

This is our first obstacle; we have no way of processing the makeup of the spiritual realm. We may mentally acknowledge that it is bigger and more real than the physical realm, but we have no context to help us relate to it. We are so used to relating to the reality of the physical realm through our five senses and our intellect that we struggle to grasp the reality of the spiritual realm which gives us no such physical cues.

The two worlds in "The Truman Show" were both physical. In contrast only one world in "The Adam Show" is physical—yet the other "spiritual" world is of such magnificence and so stunning in its reality that it relegates the physical realm to mere shadow status.

Truman left one physical reality for a bigger, truer, physical reality. But he didn't need to recalibrate his perceptions to move out of Seahaven into the big wide world—both worlds were made of the same stuff; both were perceived by his senses and intellect.

We, however, are confronted with a bigger challenge than Truman as we come to grips with our alternative reality, we can't see it yet deep inside we know we are made for it. We were pre-wired by God to live in eternity. It is stamped on our hearts, and once we catch our first glimpse of it, our hearts are forever beckoned and drawn towards its wonder and splendour.

Okay, stick with me. Even though this sounds a bit complicated, it's not—and it is so worth the effort of thinking it all through.

As we go along, I will draw some comparisons between Truman and us, his world and ours. I will use the situation in which Truman found himself to illustrate the situation we are in; and just like Truman, we don't even realise we are living out our lives in a world that is not what it seems.

To get the ball rolling, let's take a look at the way things were in the beginning.

CHAPTER 2

The Beginning

We read in Genesis that God made man "in his own image," and more than that, He made the whole of His creation perfectly. Everything that He made reflected His own nature; it was the ultimate expression of divinity, God's best work on His very best day ever. Nothing was left to chance, nothing was forgotten, it was the perfection of the most loving, life-giving being imaginable—He poured the essence of Himself into this work, held nothing back, and humanity was the pinnacle of it all.

This was the world that Adam knew at the beginning. This was his space. He spent all of his time in this perfection, and he knew nothing else.

The duality of separate worlds had not yet appeared; it was not two perfect worlds side-by-side, but one perfectly blended spiritual/physical environment. Perfection couldn't be limited to the spiritual realm only, how could a love so freely expressed have boundaries? It is unthinkable to contemplate the notion that God separated Himself in some way from His heart's expression, that He kept a comfortable distance between Himself and His creation. Never! Adam knew God as well as he knew himself; divinity and eternity were the everyday stuff of Adam's existence.

The spiritual and physical realms existed in seamless harmony for Adam; they were one big reality that he enjoyed without limit or conscious thought—God was his environment, God was in and through everything, and He was even in Adam too.

This is the reason why Paul uses such graphic language to explain the accomplishments of the cross of Jesus—we are seated in heavenly places, citizens of heaven, entering boldly…he was pulling our thinking back to God's original design.

Imagine that—living in a world where the realm of the spirit and the realm of nature are so blended that Adam didn't even need to consciously process the difference. He didn't need to mentally find a context to help him relate to God. God was a part of him, and he was a part of God because he was born of God—their union of hearts was so undivided that he was just naturally God-conscious.

The seamlessness of this amazing union was held together by just one thing, God's heart of love. His divine love poured forth from His being in a continuous, relentless flow that held Adam securely in divine bliss—all Adam had to do was lean back into God's love and revel in it.

That kind of love can only flow freely when there is nothing in its way. God's loving nature, the essence of His being, expressed itself without limit because that's who God is. As far is God is concerned, the flow is always on; the only way it won't flood over and through the object of His love is if it is blocked out by the loved one.

The concept of "Father" is in this, and the sentiment of "Papa" too. Imagine a grandchild crawling up onto its grandfather's lap and leaning back into his love; this thought beautifully captures the union as both Papa and child enjoy the pleasure of their unfettered love for each other.

> **Nothing else matters;**
> **no earthly task comes close to this ultimate expression of love.**
> **It is the full realization of their individual being,**
> **and it joins them into oneness as nothing else can.**

All of this background about Adam's original world is very important. Without a clear understanding of the way things were in the beginning, we can never fully understand the restorative work that Christ accomplished on the cross. We are more likely to interpret the reality of Christ's work through the lens of our present environment (we relate to what we can see), much as Truman could only build his identity on the basis of the environment in which he found himself.

At this point a biblical reference might be useful:

Ephesians 1:18-20 is a good place to start: *"I ask that the eyes of your heart may be enlightened, so that you may know the hope of His calling, the riches of His glorious inheritance in the saints, and the surpassing greatness of His power to us who believe. He displayed this power in the working of His mighty strength, which He exerted in Christ when He raised Him from the dead and seated Him at His right hand in the heavenly realms."*

Why would Paul pray such a prayer? He seems to be saying that we need to see into a reality different from the one before our natural eyes, a reality which views the riches, might and power of God. He doesn't pray that God would create a new reality for us, or that we would enter into a reality we aren't already in—only that we would see this present-tense spiritual reality with the eyes of our hearts.

It's as if Paul was saying, "You are living in two worlds; it's just that you can't see one of them." These two worlds already exist, and you and I are in them both. We are like Truman who also lived in two worlds and could only see one of them; he had to choose to respond to his inner voice and seek out the unseen world just as we do.

If you are a Christian these two worlds are already the fact of your life, whether you can see them both is another matter.

And that's the point of this book. In fact, it's the reason why Christ came—He came to restore to us the lost realm of God's love. To "see with the eyes of our heart" is the greatest ambition a Christian can have; it is the re-opening of our inner sight. It's more important than evangelism, charity, or any area of ministry—because our service can only be the overflow of living in the realm of God's extravagant love.

CHAPTER 3

The Dome

The dome over Seahaven Island was an artificial sky. It was a curved screen onto which Truman's false aerial environment was projected. Daytime, nighttime, good weather and bad were all projected onto the dome above Truman. The projected image rarely represented the conditions in the outer world; it could have been clear skies in the area surrounding Seahaven Island, but that had no effect on Truman's observations under the dome. Truman saw life as it was projected at him—not as it really was.

We can see things as they really are only with the eyes of our heart. The natural realm displays a reality that is very compelling and overwhelming, but it is only a small part of the truth. The realm of God, our true home which Christ restored back to us, will be obstructed by the artificial dome of self-consciousness erected over us by Adam unless we respond to the divine longing inside each of us. This call is the ancient recollection of God's unfettered love; it resonates in our spiritual memory and draws us to venture beyond the man-made dome and into the greater life for which we were really made.

Can you see it? Can you see Eternity?

It's right there—the reality of the love-union Adam shared with God is within us right now.

So let's look more closely at Adam's artificial dome.

The extravagance of God's love is not in question. We know that *"God so loved the world..."* and we know that He *"changes not,"* yet the actions of Adam resulted in a change in regard to the reality he observed. In effect Adam's actions erected an artificial dome over mankind—not a dome of God's making, but a dome of Adam's making. *God doesn't do domes!*

It's easy to jump to the conclusion that God separated Himself from Adam because He couldn't look upon his sin, but what if that conclusion is wrong?

What if that conclusion is based on the view of things from Adam's perspective, not God's?

The dome that separates humanity from God is a completely different matter if we choose to view it from man's perspective, rather than God's. Such a dome would be the observations of fallen humanity, rather than the perceptions of the eternal God. We have always assumed that our view of the problem between God and mankind is the same as God's view, but nothing could be further from the truth—God sees things very differently than man does. The fallen thinking of humanity has obscured the truth.

It's not that the dome that separates us is an illusion, or a figment of our imagination, not at all; it is very real and very relevant. So this is not merely about fine-tuning our perceptions; it is about rebuilding our understanding from the ground up so that we see things as God does.

The nature of Adam changed when he sinned, and his perceptions of reality changed with it. Everything about Adam's existence changed at that point in time. He lost his godly innocence and noticed that he was naked; his eyes were indeed opened just as satan had promised. They were opened to a see a reality at polar opposites to the reality he had known before. Not merely that there were consequences for his sin, but that his entire world had undergone a quantum shift; there was now an unfamiliar ceiling over him—he was stuck in the physical realm and his identity reflected that fact.

Yet, strangely, nothing had actually changed other than the fact that a dome of human self-consciousness had been lowered over his life.

Imagine having God's continuous and freely given love, favour, and blessing one minute, and the next minute having to earn it through human effort. From God's perspective nothing had changed, God couldn't turn off His giving nature; it was who He was. But from Adam's perspective everything had changed, the definition of his life had gone from "free access to God's world," to "limited access based on his performance on the stage of good and evil."

Adam constructed an artificial dome between himself and God, the dome of self-made worth. Prior to this, Adam's worth was entirely based on God's love for him (he was the object of love of the greatest being ever)—but after this, he had to claw his way into God's favour by his management of the good and evil equation.

Adam couldn't get to God without presenting God with his best efforts and religious rituals.

To say that this was a dramatic difference is to understate the thing; Adam had re-defined himself and his whole world—all for the chance to be independent.

The saddest part of all is that, in the process, he redefined God too. Not that Adam had the capacity to change who God was, but rather, that by adopting a lifestyle-based relationship with God, he limited God's expression of His true self. The extravagance of God's love was now conditional upon man's behaviour. Adam limited God to such a degree that the extravagance of the heart and nature of God was effectively lost to him.

> *Adam handed to God a new world order:*
> *"this is how it works down here now."*

Adam re-made God in his own limited, fallen image. Idolatry was born. Adam worshipped a God who was so scaled down that, for all intents and purposes, this God was a just a fraction of His former self as it related to life on planet earth. All of this limiting was the result of Adam's decision to redefine himself as one who could self-generate righteousness, rather than receive it for free from the overflow of God's heart of love.

Adam limited the extravagant heart of God to a man-sized commodity.

He scaled himself up, and he scaled God down, and the dome of separation was set in place. The seamlessness of God's original creation was now broken into two realms, and the perfect union that once existed between the spiritual and the physical became an ever-diminishing echo from the past.

The realm of freely given love and the realm of earned love couldn't coexist.

This separation had no initiative of God in it. Even the notion that God judged Adam is flawed; the only judging that can be apportioned to God is a direct result of Adam's choice to redefine God according to humanity's fallen nature. Nothing could have been further from God's heart than judging humanity according to their place on the scale of good and evil. The system God devised (if you can call it a system) was so superior to the system of "man-generated worthiness" that it looked like kindergarten in comparison. God's way was that He gave us holiness for free because of His incomparable love.

Make no mistake, the dome between humanity and God is entirely of man's making.

CHAPTER 4
The System Under The Dome

The entire system that governs the world is also of man's making. The fundamental assumptions that control and direct our daily lives on planet earth make no sense at all to the mind of God. To be judged, then rewarded or punished, according to the good and evil we produce is completely foreign to His heart and to His original design.

Yet, Adam's actions put God in that box.

We Christians have developed much of our understanding of God according to the fallen thinking of Adam. God judged humanity while we were all still under the spell of Adam's curse, only because that was the environment Adam chose for us. But Jesus came to release us back to our original design so that we can once again live as those who are carried aloft by the freedom of the Spirit, not weighed down by the obligations of the rulebook.

This statement does not diminish in any way the importance of living decent and good lives; rather, it lifts us to the place where we can actually do it by remaining and abiding in His love.

There is a lot to discuss regarding the difference between Adam's thinking and God's, and Adam's perceptions of reality and God's. The few pages given to the subject so far are insufficient to do the scale of the issue justice, so we will continue to reach back and unpack it as the book unfolds. The important thing right now is to consider the notion that we may be perceiving truth in a way that is quite different to God's view of things.

I was told growing up that what separated me from God was my sin. While it is true that my sin is a factor, the real problem is that I have inherited Adam's nature and have inserted my behaviour and Christian lifestyle as the means for receiving God's freely given love.

We know from John 15:26 *that "the Spirit testifies about Christ"*—but the fallen nature of Adam wants the Spirit to testify about us. We want the Spirit to report to God how well we are doing. This is what grieves the Holy Spirit—not so much that I sin, but that I depend on my own self-righteousness, which is the epitome of all sin.

The reality God sees is that Christ's righteousness has made me worthy—the inferior reality that I received from Adam is that I am not worthy until I bring my life into alignment with God's expectations.

So I must choose one.

These two are exclusive and cannot be blended. John 6:63 says; *"The Spirit gives life, the flesh counts for nothing"*—unless I choose to believe that the Spirit gives life, I am choosing by default the limitations of the flesh.

The flesh wants to break through the artificial dome by pushing human virtue in God's face; the flesh wants God to re-value human effort as equal with Godly righteousness. But this was Adam's approach, and God will have none of it. The dome can be penetrated only from the top down. It has always been that way—God gives life, and we receive it from Him.

> *Jesus deconstructed the dome;*
> *He came to give us God's life again.*

Jesus did more than pay the price for our sin; He removed our self-made separation from His Father.

So the dome that separates us from God is not sin *per se,* but our state of independence from God's free gift of life. Religion drives us on, as we attempt to please God by presenting Him with our lifestyle when He is already pleased with us because Christ has made us worthy. Sinful living is simply the result of our attempts to self-generate a right standing with God instead of receiving it as a gift.

It's important to see and understand the Genesis story with fresh eyes if we are to lay hold of this. There are a few main players to keep our eyes on: God, Adam, Eve, satan, the Tree of Life, and the Tree of the Knowledge of Good and Evil.

God created a perfect world for Adam and Eve and the entire human race that would follow. It was a perfect world without fault of any kind, created for His loved ones who were also without stain or wrinkle or any other blemish—they were holy and blameless. We read in Ephesians 5:27 how Jesus restored us to our originally created design.

The perfection of God's original creation is the same perfection as Christ's gift of redemption— we have been redeemed back to the original.

Satan proposed an alternative to Adam and Eve; he offered them a new kind of sight, one that shifted the focus away from their spiritual bliss and toward an awareness previously unknown to them—the knowledge of good and evil. This awareness would position them for a different kind of existence, a god-like existence where they would control their destiny by their own deeds and choices. The knowledge of good and evil would become the source of their existence; it would light their way along life's journey. Genesis 3:4-7 lays it out for us.

There were two trees of particular interest in the Garden of Eden—the Tree of Life, and the Tree of the Knowledge of Good and Evil.

Jesus is life—*"I am the way, the truth, and the life"* (John 14:6). And He came to give life—*"I came that they may have life"* (John 10:10). Jesus and the Tree of Life are the same divine life source. It is spiritual life, flowing without limit from the heart of God to His loved ones. Revelation 2:7 tells us that the Tree of Life is in the Paradise of God—the garden of God's delight.

The Tree of Life was in Paradise, and it represents the divine, life-giving nature of God in the eternal realm.

The Tree of the Knowledge of Good and Evil refers to a different kind of life source based in the physical realm. By eating from it, Adam and Eve chose and entered into a new reality where they were subjected to the loss of their Godly innocence, and ultimately death. Their new existence delivered to them a dependence on their performance in the physical realm; everything became connected to their conduct—whether good or evil. There was no spiritual life in this existence; it was a physical existence based entirely on the man-generated currency of human behaviour. If a man worked hard or was shrewd or resourceful, he could expect a life of good things; if, on the other hand, he was lazy and didn't make the most of his opportunities, then it could go very badly for him.

It was the exact opposite of God's design.

There was only one thing that man couldn't buy with human effort—spiritual life, the life that God gives. Spiritual life was given freely from the heart of God, and Jesus came to give it to us. Jesus came to give us back that which the actions of Adam and Eve had taken from us.

Adam thought he could have both; he thought he could live in two worlds at the same time with human effort as the currency. He believed he could gather up the fruit he had produced from his diligent efforts labouring at the Tree of the Knowledge of Good and Evil and present this fruit to God to gain access to the Tree of Life. But God said, "No, you can't buy My love. It is not a commodity that can be purchased; I cannot change My nature just because you decided to change yours."

We read in Genesis 3:22-24 how God banished Adam from the Tree of Life. He posted an angelic guard between paradise and the earth (between the spiritual and physical realms) so that Adam could not access God's gift of life through his self-generated morality. The two realms, once magnificently and seamlessly unified, were separated by the dome of human self-sufficiency.

This dome created an environment over mankind between the period of time from Adam to Christ, but it no longer exists in our day. Jesus came to earth and released His life back into the hearts of men and women. He effectively relieved the angelic guard from duty and threw open the gates of heaven to all who would come. Now, there is no dome; nothing separates us from the love of God. We have full and unrestricted access to all that is found in the kingdom of God. All of God's love, favour and blessing are once again ours as we place faith in Jesus.

Of course, if we think the dome remains in place by perpetuating Adam's independently generated self-worth, then for us it does remain in place. If we insist on redefining God just like Adam did, then God can do no more for us than what is already done. The eyes of our hearts have the ability to see all the way into the realm of the Spirit; we are re-connected. All that remains is that we agree with God and live confidently in the new identity Jesus has given us.

We will talk in more detail about "the eyes of the heart" later, but for now think of it this way: the eyes of our hearts give us a view into heaven (the very realm of God); they take in the invisible realm of the Spirit by faith. It is much more than simply an enhanced operation of our natural sight;

in fact, it is not at all like our natural sight. Rather, it is a conviction of the heart, which enables us to treat the invisible realities as though they are visible.

CHAPTER 5
Spiritual Sight

Several times in the Bible we read of a person's ability to see the invisible, but none is more clearly stated than Hebrews 11:27 which says, *"By faith... he saw him who is invisible."*

We cannot see invisible things with our natural sight, but we can confidently live in their reality by faith. In that regard, faith is not so much an action as an ability to see a different reality.

I mentioned earlier in this book that Truman could have happily remained living on Seahaven Island had he been able to see the greater reality of his existence. Seahaven Island was simply a town in which his house was located, and he could have remained living in that house if he could see it as just a part of the bigger picture. There was nothing actually wrong with living in Seahaven Island, as long as it could be viewed in its correct context as just a part of his world, and not the whole.

It's the same for us. There is nothing wrong with enjoying the created physical world we call earth. It is a magnificent expression of God's splendour. But we must see it for what it is—just a small part of the greater reality of our lives in God. We are just passing through here as temporary citizens.

Jesus purchased back our citizenship in heaven; He paid the ultimate price so that we could be relocated back into His world. But we must choose to live there; we must come to terms with the inheritance he provided for us. God cannot do more than fling wide the gates of heaven for us; He cannot force us to live as citizens of heaven. Only we can make that decision.

I am convinced that we would gladly recalibrate our concept of the realm of the Spirit if we could clearly see the magnificent scale and wonder of it. But we don't see it clearly, and so, by default, we elevate the natural realm to a status that is beyond it. The natural realm barely scratches the surface compared to the realm of God, which is our true home.

John 5:24 tells us that we have "crossed over"; we are already in eternal life. However, we don't generally live as citizens of eternity because we can't see the reality of it.

Instead, we have a theology about it. We hold it as a concept that fits neatly into our broader belief system, but it is so much more than an intellectual proposition—it is the most real fact of our existence.

God's reality is our reality—can you see it?

The dome of self-sufficiency acts like the earth's atmosphere—it deflects truth. The greater reality of God's unconditional love for us bounces off the dome's artificial atmosphere much like a meteorite bounces of the earth's atmosphere. God's love is real just like the meteorite is real; it's just that it can't reach our hearts if it must pass through the lie of humanity's self-dependence.

This is the ultimate intention of satan; he knew that he couldn't change God (which was his actual intention all along), so instead he has changed us (the objects of God's love)—so much so that our perception of God is deformed by the atmosphere of self we have placed in front of Him.

When we perceive God through the lens of our acceptability by way of lifestyle and religion, we allow satan the lie; we become unwitting participants in the greatest travesty ever—the suppression of God's true identity.

The essence of God's nature is that He is love. His identity is so intrinsically woven into His heart of love that we diminish His reality in our lives when we place limits over His expression of that love. It's not that we change God; He cannot be changed. But we can obstruct the expression of His love when we introduce our behaviour as the mechanism that releases it. In so doing, God ceases to be His true self as it relates to us—and satan revels in his mischief.

God is not waiting for us to confess a sin, have a quiet time, or enter into worship so that his loving nature can be expressed to us—we are always saturated in His love.

If satan can alter our view of God, then he takes great pleasure in the accomplishment.

CHAPTER 6
Self-Conscious

Jesus explained to the woman at the well in John 4:24 that, *"God is spirit, and his worshippers must worship in spirit and in truth."* It is this that satan has attempted to unsettle—he has diminished our perspective of God to the extent that we cease to worship Him in spirit and in truth and end up worshipping a god that we have scaled down to our own image.

How have we scaled Him down? We have limited Him to the human way—we have determined that *He* cannot express His love to us unless we present Him with our personal best; and we have also determined that *we* cannot relate to Him other than in the context of our earth-bound ideas. In other words, we want Him to express His "god-ness" by being engaged in our earthly circumstances, rather than by giving His life to our spirits.

Can you see? God is diminished by our obsession with our earth-based issues, when in fact; His accomplishment in restoring our spiritual condition was actually our greatest issue. We attempt to pull God down to our realm instead of relocating our identity into His kingdom and the security of His love.

Don't get me wrong—our physical needs are very real and pressing. But unless we see them in perspective, they will overwhelm us. Jesus Himself said, *"In this world you will have trouble, but take heart, I have overcome the world."* He wasn't being callous or neglectful; He was being honest—our only lasting relief from the pressures of this life is found by resting in His eternal, surpassing love.

God is not 'issue focused'; that would be Adam's way. Adam limited God to "engaging in our earthly problems as they arise"—because he had remade his identity out of the good and evil he produced. God is *life* focused; He came that we might have life abundantly. He said to the Jewish leaders in John 5:40, *"You refuse to come to me to have life."*

The divine order in this is that we must come to Jesus and receive life (spiritual life) before we approach Him with our physical needs. The dome of the good and evil mentality of humanity can perceive only our earthly needs (the realm of the spirit is hidden from view). Yet it is in the realm of the Spirit that our true identity is found.

> *Our real security cannot be constructed out of*
> *whether our earthly circumstances are pleasing to us;*
> *it can be built only upon whether*
> *we are secure in the unconditional love of God.*

This is probably the saddest aspect of today's modern Christian culture—people are directed to pull God into their prosperity, health and relationship issues, instead of first lifting people above their earthly needs to rest in God's heart of love.

We are told to pray more and longer, to cry out to God, to study the Bible intensely, and doggedly apply its principles—as if God is stuck in a divine inertia until we motivate Him by our spiritual aerobics. Do we really think that God depends on a man-made physical activity to release a spiritual blessing?

We have become so *un*accustomed to resting in the loving nature of God that we find it disturbing to simply ease back and let God be God. So compelling is the artificial reality we have of God that we have lost the knack of confidently embracing His love for fear that we might offend His divine expectations of us. It has become normal for us to hide from God's love.

Adam and Eve did it as their first response to God after eating from the wrong tree; they hid from the great lover of their souls because they were afraid of Him. But why? They had nothing to fear; God hadn't changed… *they had*. God's love continued to flow unabated towards them; they just couldn't see it through their self-conscious shame.

They saw for the first time a performance-based view of everything. It was like pulling the blinds down over God's unconditional love and substituting a false reality in its place. And now we have lived for so long in this false reality that it has become the new normal.

The Genesis story of Adam and Eve's demise is not a very long narrative; in fact we get only half of one verse to deal with the change to their reality as they perceived it. Other consequences resulted, but this is the only thing recorded that Adam and Eve initially observed: *"Then the eyes of both of them were opened, and they realized they were naked"* (Genesis 3:7a).

They were naked before they sinned, and it didn't cause them any concern; but as soon as their eyes were opened, their condition in the physical context became the measure of their identity. God didn't care if they were naked; He made them that way. And they didn't care either until the eyes of their flesh took over the job previously performed by the eyes of their heart.

> ***Their identity was based on their physical condition,***
> ***not their status as the beloved of God.***

This is the outcome of choosing to live on the basis of good and evil—we become self-conscious instead of God-conscious. We gauge our value on the basis of our performance on the stage of lifestyle and religion, instead of on the basis of God's unconditional love for us. In other words, we take that which was unconditional and add conditions to it.

CHAPTER 7

Identity

Everything in life overflows from our identity, and if we base our identity on earthly values and outcomes, then we are destined to a life of slavery to man-pleasing duties. When we choose to construct our identity in that way, everything we are and do is pre-empted by the word *enough*—Have I done well enough? Do I look good enough? Am I spiritually active enough or good enough for God? Do I pray enough and read my Bible enough?

We weren't designed to live this way. We were designed to gain all of our confidence from God's heart, not our own performance; yet most of us have grown up being told to measure our value on the basis of our actions and appearance.

Humanity has lived for so long under the shadow of this performance-based identity that we can't imagine the alternative. Like Truman, we know no other way; it has become the truth of our existence and, as a result, we live our lives as only a fraction of our true selves. The umbrella of our self-consciousness is keeping out the thing we want most—God's pleasure and delight. We have been told that we need this umbrella to protect us from God's wrath, but that's just the lie satan has been pushing for thousands of years. Our determination to approach God on the basis of our personal best is actually keeping out His personal best.

Can you see this? It comes as quite a shock at first, to learn that God doesn't operate like we do.

Adam thought that God was mad at him, so he and Eve hid behind a tree—but nothing could have been further from the truth. God continued to love Adam unconditionally and had even planned his salvation at great personal cost before Adam and Eve had even sinned.

> *We must become comfortable with the extravagance of God, else we remain on the hamster wheel of self-consciousness.*

God will always be true to His great love for us; our part is to let Him.

For the most part, humanity has not let God be true to Himself. We have told Him who to be, instead of resting in His good nature. We have changed our identity and then told God to get with the program.

So it is essential that we get the issue of identity sorted out—it changes everything.

The Bible doesn't use the term *identity* much; it is a modern term. But it speaks of identity consistently, page after page. God declared His identity loud and clear when He called Himself 'I am', and Jesus followed suit in John 8:58: *"Truly, truly, I say to you, before Abraham was born, I am."* Their identity was bigger than this world—it was based in eternity.

The apostle John refers to himself five times as "the disciple whom Jesus loved" in the Gospel of John. It is not recorded anywhere else that Jesus loved John more than the others, or that Jesus coined this special name for John. So it seems that John simply referred to himself according to the identity which he felt was true. John had become so completely clothed in Jesus' love that it became his truest identity. John wasn't bragging or word-smithing; he was just telling it as he saw it.

Paul spoke of this in Galatians 2:20: *"I no longer live, but Christ lives in me."* This wasn't a mission statement based on his unique calling; it was a simple fact—Paul had lost himself in the reality of Christ.

And then in Ephesians and Colossians, Paul applies this to other believers: *"God has chosen to reveal the mystery hidden for ages—which is Christ in you."*

Adam gave us an identity based on our earthly characteristics, activities and accomplishments—and Jesus has given us back the heavenly identity for which we were designed.

Who are you?

Are you the sum of your earth-bound existence, or are you the vessel into which Jesus has poured God's love and life?

CHAPTER 8

The Spirit

Jesus said in John 6:63, *"The Spirit gives life, the flesh counts for nothing."* We must stop looking to the flesh for our identity and learn to lean in to the divine nature of God, our new born-again self.

If I refuse the identity Christ came to give me, then I elevate the work of Adam above the work of Jesus. We would never deliberately do such a thing, yet that is the truth of the matter. By seeing ourselves as anything less than the righteousness of God, we are declaring loud and clear that Adam succeeded in defining us, and Jesus failed.

Sadly we are more likely to see ourselves as identified in the failed experiment of Adam than the victorious mission of Jesus because our human weaknesses and failings are always before us. So we must look beyond the weaknesses of the flesh to the life of the Spirit and declare loud and clear, "I am who God says I am."

There is no victory in Adam's way; it is a vicious cycle that continues till we die unless we jump off that cycle and land in Christ. Then we can say, "I no longer live, but Christ lives in me," or perhaps "The Spirit came to give me life, and my flesh died in the process."

No Christian would deliberately grieve the Holy Spirit. John 15:26 says, *"The Holy Spirit testifies about Jesus,"* yet we do exactly what we don't want to do and grieve the Holy Spirit when we choose the testimony of Adam above the testimony of Jesus. We grieve the Holy Spirit because we call His testimony a lie. Adam declares that we are failures who have attempted to please God and fallen short; Jesus declares that He has made us worthy apart from our personal failures.

Who will we believe?

The Holy Spirit does not testify about Adam; He testifies about Jesus. That is why Jesus sent Him to us from the Father; and we individually choose whether to believe or dismiss that testimony.

The Holy Spirit does not testify that Jesus got the ball rolling, and we finish the job by adding our own virtuous life. Quite the contrary, the Holy Spirit testifies that Jesus completed the job all by Himself in spite of us. The Holy Spirit declares that Jesus has set us free into the life of the Spirit; it is up to us to accept that truth and turn our backs on the flesh as the source of our security.

When Jesus said, "The Spirit gives life, the flesh counts for nothing," He was referring to our identity. He was telling us to receive the life of the Spirit and stop trying to impress God with works of the flesh. Works of the flesh are of value in the economy of the realm under the dome, but they count for nothing in the realm of God—for that, only the unconditional love of God expressed in the gift of Jesus counts.

Imagine the value of the unconditional love of God as a trillion dollars, and the value of our self-made worth as one cent—it simply isn't relevant in the scheme of things. Yet religion has taught us that God is looking over the banisters of heaven inspecting our personal best, weighing it in the balance and deciding if it is enough to tip the scales in our favour. It's a scam. God simply looks at whether we place faith in Jesus as our complete source of life—and if we do, then the inspection is over, and we pass with flying colours.

Adam invented this whole inspection process when he chose the Tree of the Knowledge of Good and Evil, but God wasn't in it. He was in the Tree of Life. God didn't give the human race the law and the Ten Commandments because He wanted them to measure up to His standards; He did it because they had chosen the "inspection process," and His only option was to clearly articulate for them what they had chosen.

If it was God's initiative that we have the law and the Ten Commandments, then it follows that God wanted to give us death and not life (because we can never measure up to it). However, Jesus says in John 10:10, *"I came to give you life abundantly."* God will never jump on board with Adam's agenda; it isn't in Him—and it is grossly offensive to His love that religion keeps insisting on it.

To clarify, religion can be defined as humanity attempting to please God through various rituals, practices and protocols; in contrast, faith is believing that Jesus qualifies us to enjoy God's pleasure without bringing any personal quality or action. You can see then why Adam and Eve felt naked once they had adopted good and evil as the measure of their identity; and ultimately, religion was the culmination of attempting to impress God on the basis of their personal best.

CHAPTER 9

The Mind Of Adam

The notion that God is not inspecting our lives is a big hurdle for the mind of Adam to jump, and also for us who have inherited his thinking. We are so entrenched in the system that was developed around Adam's thinking that it seems impossible for us to think otherwise. Yet there is an ancient longing in us that yearns for a different way—a way that is based on something higher than the rat race, a way that is truly free of the daily grind of measuring up.

You might be thinking, "If Adam lost sight of God's unconditional love, how am I ever going to see it? I am of Adam's family tree and can't see the divine realities any more than he could."

This would be true were it not for Jesus.

Jesus ended Adam's genealogy—Jesus was the last Adam. For those of us that follow, a new family line has been established; we are the sons and daughters of God not Adam. That's what the term "born again" means; we have been re-born into God's family, we have His nature coursing through us—we are born of God. The period between Adam and Jesus was populated by descendants of Adam, and the period since Jesus has been populated by descendants of God—and all that is required by us is that we personally believe it.

Think back to Truman; as true as the big, wide world was, it was not true for Truman until he believed it was true. And that's the problem for us, too; we are not used to assigning truth to anything unless it is accompanied by physical proof. We must accept that the realm of the spirit does not operate that way; the spiritual man believes in a reality which is greater than the physical realm, yet not accompanied by evidence we can touch or see.

The evidence of the spirit begins in our hearts;
it is a deep longing for God which propels us to do the unthinkable
—to hand our existence over to the care of one we cannot see
and entrust ourselves to an unconditional love which defies human logic.

There are some who attempt this as a leap into the unknown; they risk all and hope that God will be there to catch them. They take their religious thinking all the way to its limits by assuming that God is looking for a bold act to which He can give His support.

But this new kind of trust is not a leap into the unknown; it is a leap into the safest truth we can ever know. To the religious mind, it seems like an unknown because the religious man looks for physical evidence to prove that God can be trusted; but to the spiritual man, it is the absolute truth of his life because he has examined the claims of the cross of Christ and determined that he can entrust himself into it. Like Truman, the spiritual man has decided long before he steps out that the cross of Christ is the most compelling truth in history.

This is not about our religious fervour;
it is about the truth of God's eternal love.

The remarkable thing about this truth is that it begins in the heart and slowly works its way into our head. It cannot make sense in the head first, because it is not an intellectual concept; rather it is a deep and profound realization within us which we cannot shake off. Adam remade humanity with a truth meter that looked for physical and intellectual evidence—but Jesus remade us back to our origins to look past the physical evidence and into the heart of God. The Bible calls it "the eyes of the heart."

Once we see the truth with the eyes of the heart, a strange thing begins to take place; we discover that our intellect falls into line. What previously seemed completely irrational takes on a new and higher rationality all its own.

Even this process cannot be fully explained in rational, intellectual terms; it is above the earthly truth, which has been neatly constrained within physical proof by Adam's view of things. And we lay hold of it by a sight that is divine, not mortal. In short, don't expect God to function in the box that religion has made for Him—He is surprising, extravagant and without earthly limitations. It's beautifully summed up for us in Isaiah 55:9. *"As the heavens are higher than the earth, so are my ways higher than your ways and my thoughts than your thoughts."*

Amazingly, God hasn't left us floundering around in the ways of the earth; He has lifted us up to His ways and given us the mind of Christ (1 Corinthians 2:16).

CHAPTER 10

God's Logic

Now that we are beginning to understand the difference between these two realms, we can see that they each operate on a completely different basis. We can't bring the logic of the earth and overlay it onto the Kingdom of God and expect it to function in the same way. We must leave behind the world's *modus operandi* when we stake our claim in the realm of God; the world's ways bring no trading power to the deal.

This is where we make a departure from the example of Truman. He moved between two worlds that essentially operated on the same basis. In contrast the Kingdom of God bears absolutely no resemblance to the earthly realm—not because God designed it that way, but because Adam shifted the balance by choosing the Tree of the Knowledge of Good and Evil. The original model that God designed had His heart of love filling us with life, like a river of divine goodness that satisfied us in every way. Adam turned this one directional river into a two-lane highway that depended on both parties to maintain the flow.

Adam took the most sublime fact of human existence and mixed it with his compulsive need to earn his own way, with the result that the magnificence of God's nature has been watered down to a trickle. The heart of God is not mean-spirited or miserly; it is abundant and extravagant in ways that we cannot imagine—and God simply awaits our faith in His true nature to have that river flow freely again.

Jesus said that He came to give us life abundantly, and that divine life awaits us all if we will simply believe that God is as good as He claims to be.

In Ephesians 3:14-21 Paul gives us a glimpse of this: *"For this reason I kneel before the Father, from whom every family in heaven and on earth derives its name. I pray that out of his glorious riches he may strengthen you with power through his Spirit in your inner being, so that Christ may dwell in your hearts through faith. And I pray that you, being rooted and established in love, may have power, together with all the Lord's holy people, to grasp how wide and long and high and deep is the love of Christ, and to know this love that surpasses knowledge—that you may be filled to the measure of all the fullness of God. Now to him who is able to do immeasurably more than all we ask or imagine, according to his power that is at work within us, to him be glory in the church and in Christ Jesus throughout all generations, for ever and ever! Amen."*

Paul wants to stretch our imagination all the way out to its limits, and then take it even further—he wants us to take off the filtered view we have of God and grasp his surpassing, immeasurable, extravagance. To do less is to limit God to our earthly normality... *we really don't want to do that.*

This amazing portion of Scripture didn't appear in the Bible by mistake; it is Paul's prayer for us (the church). Paul was possibly the man with the greatest revelation of the gospel to ever walk the earth, and he considered these words to be the epitome of human existence.

> **If our religious activities**
> **obscure the stunning spectacle which is the love of God,**
> **then we are barely alive at all.**

God said to Adam and Eve, "Don't eat from the Tree of the Knowledge of Good and Evil because if you do, you will surely die"—and to live without the lavish security of the love of God is to barely be alive at all. It is the death of our true selves—creatures made for His love, deliberately measuring it according to their earthly performance.

How sad.

What a tragedy, to have such a bountiful gift and to partake so sparingly.

The dome over us that has the greatest impact on our lives is not the sky. It is not the air that surrounds us. It is the limit we have placed upon the nature of the one who loves us most.

We could easily become quite morbid as we contemplate the scale of this agonizing miscarriage of the truth, but we mustn't. Listen again to the heart of God: *"Let us fix our eyes on Jesus, the author and perfecter of our faith, who for the joy set before him he endured the cross, scorning its shame, and sat down at the right hand of the throne of God."*

In the midst of all the pain and suffering, Jesus saw a joyful future that enabled Him to endure it all. It was a future that saw us revelling again in the love of God—just like He made us to do in the first place.

Wow! I can no longer accommodate the meagre view of God that I knew under the dome. He is so much more than I thought, and He yearns for me with all of His God-sized heart.

It blows the top off all my preconceptions of God that made up the artificial truth contained within the dome of my religious thinking. Now that I have finally poked my head through the clouds and viewed God for who He really is, I realise I've been playing childish games with Him—containing Him in the safety of my shrunken mindset. And I'm not alone. All of us who have become secure in religion have limited God to our petty, self-obsessed thinking.

The God that I used to speculate about wasn't the surpassing, immeasurable kind of God that Paul describes; He was unsurpassing and limited just like me. In some respects, He was me; He was a figment of my own self-styled thinking.

I fell for it, I swallowed the lie hook, line and sinker—satan put a view of God before me that fit nicely into my insecure little world, and I embraced it as my own. For much of my life, I worshipped an idol—a god I had constructed in my own meagre image, because I had no idea He was immeasurably more. Sure, I gave lip service to the greatness of God, but it didn't overwhelm me like it should have. So in reality, it was nothing more than adherence to a religious ideal.

Just because ninety percent of the Christian population have no compelling interest in personally discovering life on the other side of the dome doesn't make it any less real. Truth is truth, and the gate that leads to life is narrow and few find it, but we can't close our eyes to this greater reality just because there is no human stampede towards it. The truth is what God says, not the limited view of the masses, and we get only one life to agree with God.

When we get to heaven, we will see God as He is; and this sight will cause us to become like Him, as we are told in 1 John 3:2. But wouldn't it be better to see Him as He is now and become like Him in real time?

CHAPTER 11
A Scaled-Down God

Let me tell you a bit more about the downsized version of God that I carried with me for most of my life. He was God, so He was different than us—but also remarkably like us (the human race). He was a grandfatherly type who mixed wisdom with love and looked over His spectacles with fondness at we mortals who were doing our best. He was sort of benevolently distant—not so much distracted as preoccupied with matters that were beyond me. I knew He loved me, and occasionally I imagined Him bouncing me on His knee. But He spent most of His time in His study thinking big thoughts that didn't involve me.

Prayer was always something of a juggling act; I found myself approaching God with a certain amount of confidence because I knew He loved me, but also doubting myself because of my less-than-perfect life, *which He knew all about.* Added to that was a lot of uncertainty about how it all worked. Plenty of people seemed to know all the answers, but it didn't translate into a process with which I felt entirely comfortable. So I treated God in much the same way that I treated my earthly grandpa—I dropped in occasionally and didn't give Him too much information.

All in all, I didn't see God how He was; I saw Him how I was.

That wasn't actually too hard for me to do because I was a relatively good guy. I was as good as the next guy, and probably better than many others, so I figured that I was well positioned to get a handle on God. I was a clear thinker, people liked me, and I was fully engaged in church life—so that qualified me to confidently determine and articulate who God was. You might say that because I had my life "together," it followed that I had God "together." In that regard, my God was simply the overflow of me!

It all came down to my perceptions of reality. My entire existence was contained within the dome of an artificial earth-bound reality, but to me this reality was the whole picture. It was like a filter through which everything had to pass, including God. I filtered the truth about God through the physical reality of my earthly circumstances and environmental issues; I saw Him as an extension of my life on earth. I considered this artificial reality to be so mandatory and binding on me, that it became the primary truth through which every other truth must be interpreted, including God.

For instance; if my circumstances were pleasing to me, then I assumed that this was an indication that God was happy with me; conversely, if my circumstances were troubling, then I assumed God was unhappy with me or perhaps correcting some characteristic in me which required fine tuning.

It never occurred to me that I should reverse the equation and put the truth about God first. He is unconditionally loving, and if my circumstances were causing me difficulty, then all I had to do was rest in His love to experience peace and joy again. Sure my circumstances are real and at times difficult, but the greater reality of God's endless flow of love and life is my most authentic truth.

I guess you could say that I had to choose my primary address, the place of my true habitation—was I living in God, or was I living in the issues of life on earth? In John 17:14 Jesus says that His disciples are *"not of this world any more than he is of this world."* My challenge was to learn how to live in the greater reality about which Jesus spoke.

As I said earlier, it all came down to my perceptions of reality—which "reality" I was choosing as my true and personal address, the reality where I actually lived.

This may seem like a mind game or perhaps some sort of esoteric manipulation, but it is nothing of the sort. I am not advocating a stretch of the imagination like a child who disappears into a make-believe world and then reappears when it is time for tea. This is more like a choice of the heart to respond to the distant call of love, and then to relocate permanently back to the ancestral home where this love is the very atmosphere we breathe.

The example provided by the Truman Show is helpful here; we do not cease to be the person we are in the natural realm, but rather we recalibrate our understanding of truth such that a shift in our identity takes place, and we begin to live as citizens of the greater realm.

*As that inner transformation takes hold,
the reality of the realm of the Spirit
overtakes the reality of the natural realm.*

Wrapping words around something so far above our normal experience is a challenge. Paul had to employ terms like *surpassing* and *immeasurable* to even scratch the surface. So I am asking you to venture beyond the bounds of our normal thinking and into the impossible. If we can't venture into the impossible, then we will remain residents of our personal Seahaven Island until the day we die and discover that there was so much more all along.

CHAPTER 12

Who Am I?

This relocation of our identity is not about doing more religious things like listening to worship music more often or getting up early for a quiet time. The shift is not sensory, emotional or intellectual; it is revelational, so we do not get there by doing more of the things that we have always done. We get there by choosing to believe rather than choosing to do—it is a journey that does not depend on self, but rather exchanges self for the indwelling Christ.

"Christ in me" is a term with which we are familiar; it is a part of the normal Christian vernacular. In my case I relegated this term to the category of useful Christian terminology; it was just another part of my extensive library of Christian enigmas, to the extent that I was robbed of its real import.

This library was compiled over a long period of time as I wandered my way through the Christian culture picking up a useful anecdote here and a wise catchphrase there, but always within the context of my limited world of self-realisation.

I didn't know there was a bigger world out there until life dealt me a blow that stopped me in my tracks long enough to catch a fresh glimpse of the cross of Christ. Even though the cross had always been the central fact of my faith, it had always had a distance about it that maintained it as more historic than personal, and the fact was that I didn't actually know how to make it personal. My faith was made up of other more personal things like going to church, attending prayer meetings and Bible studies, and just doing Christian things—so much so, that they cluttered my life like a demanding obstacle course that kept me from the cross of Jesus.

When life stopped me in my tracks, I looked up and there was the cross, radiating the love of God down through the centuries and into my heart in that very time and place. It was a revelation to me, not because I was lacking in Bible knowledge or teaching, but because I finally shifted it from my head to my heart—it ceased to be intellectual information and became my self-defining truth.

> *I finally saw that the cross was all about me,*
> *not about the religion we had built in its name.*

There is no "me" other than the "me" who was crucified with Christ. I realised it was time to shift my focus from the good (Christianity) to the best (Christ).

This is so much more than cerebral knowledge; it is the redefining of my being.

Who am I?

In the past I would have answered, "I am a Christian, a husband and father, a business man and community leader." Now I would answer, "I am the object of God's love made whole by the sacrifice of Jesus. I am not primarily defined by what I do; I am defined by God's love for me."

Who am I? I am whoever God says I am—I agree with His opinion of me.

He sees the whole picture; He sees me in the context of the restoration I experienced through the cross. He sees the whole of me, not just the limited view I get from the eyes of my flesh. *I will go with His opinion.*

This is where it gets really exciting. God has a different opinion of me than I do.

My opinion is constrained within the limited reality of my self-oriented world. My opinion is the product of the good and evil in my life; it is a collection of all of the stuff that has been handed to me by others, done by my own hands, and overflowed from the brokenness of our world. It is just a fraction of the truth of who I am, because I am also the walking, talking container of the most spectacular love and life in the universe, and beyond.

The neurons in my brain bounce around like out-of-control bugs caught in a spotlight as I try to process the real me. It is too infinite a picture to fit onto the finite screen of my life; it is too much information for me to handle, so I must find a better way to lay hold of it.

The Holy Spirit slows me down. He tells me not to overthink it because my head was not designed to deal with this kind of information—it is a thing of the heart, where the natural and the divine blend together to create a perfection beyond human understanding. The posture of the natural man is that he attempts to pull himself up to God through his cerebral understanding; he tries to contain God in his thoughts. The posture of the spiritual man is that he leans back into the love and life of God—he loses himself into the higher truth of God's goodness.

> *The natural man attempts to contain God;*
> *the spiritual man allows God to contain him.*

My brain cannot contain God. It wasn't designed for that purpose, and that also demonstrates the foolishness of Adam's mad adventure; he attempted to do a thing which was impossible for him. By choosing to be contained by his own "good and evil" life rather than the righteousness of God, he assigned to his limited intellect a task for which it wasn't qualified. His head would never come to terms with the scale and wonder of God. All he could hope for was to pull a limited image of God into his fallen world and settle for that.

CHAPTER 13

The Divine Nature

As I've said before, God cannot be minimized to fit under the dome. Remember in Exodus 33:20 when Moses asked God to show him His glory and God responded, *"You cannot see my face, for no one may see me and live."* This is the reality that confronts us; the limitations of religion and Old Covenant thinking do not give us entrée into the presence of God. For that we must venture beyond the limitations of our man-made virtue and embrace God's gift, personally laying claim to the divine nature of God as our own.

The apostle Peter didn't write too much of the Bible, just two short letters—but in 2 Peter 1:4 he makes up for his few written words by summing up the most remarkable of all truths: *"He has given us His precious and magnificent promises, so that through them we may become partakers of the divine nature."* I didn't make this up; Peter put it out there long before me. We become partakers of the divine nature.

We do not partake of the divine nature by our engagement in any culture or organization. We participate in it by personally stepping into the work of the cross of Christ, by believing it as the primary fact of our lives. And as we do, Jesus' divine nature becomes our own. The culture and organizations of Christianity may indeed be the place where this takes place, but in themselves they are not the containers of the divine nature; we are, and we individually gain it by hiding ourselves in the love of God expressed on the cross.

I have heard some people say that they let God into some of the rooms in their heart, but not all; they fear that if they let Him have full access, then He might insist on changes they don't want to make. This thinking is a perpetuation of the madness of Adam. Why would we limit the most loving being in the universe from full access to our lives? It is an "all in" proposition. When we entrust someone with our lives, there is no holding back. If we entrust only a part, then we are effectively holding back all.

Partaking of the divine nature is an all-or-nothing thing; God is not waiting around for someone to take up His offer. On the contrary, He says, "Give up your life, let it be crucified with Christ, and arise a new creation. If you are not willing to trust My love for you, then you are effectively choosing to remain under the dome of religion."

If we could just see the scale of this, we would step in in a heartbeat; but we hold back for lack of spiritual sight and continue to exist in a reality which, by comparison, is barely real at all.

Remember the Scripture in Romans 8:19, *"The creation waits in eager expectation for the revelation of the sons of God."* This is what I am talking about; there is an expectation built into creation which anticipates the moment when we embrace our true selves. The eyes of the universe are upon us, waiting in suspense to see if we will do it, hoping that we will step out and be the ones who are born of God.

John 1:12 puts it so well: *"Yet to all who received him, to those who believed in his name, he gave the right to become children of God."* He gave us the *right* when we believed in Him; now He waits for us to do it, to exercise that right and embrace our true divine-natured selves.

There is no obstacle here, but us.

CHAPTER 14

The Eyes Of The Heart

The magnificent prayer that Paul prayed for the Ephesian church recorded in Ephesians 1:18-19—*"I pray also that the eyes of your heart would be enlightened in order that you may know the hope to which he has called you, the riches of his glorious inheritance in the saints, and his incomparable power for us who believe"*—holds the key. The eyes of our heart exist. Paul doesn't ask God to give them to us; he simply prays that they be enlightened.

We are ready right now to cast our gaze over the invisible realm of the Spirit; Jesus returned to us the sight with which Adam was created. We have fully operational spiritual eyes that can view the magnificent vista which is the kingdom of God. We do not lack the spiritual ocular equipment; we just haven't made use of it for so long that we have lost the knack of doing it. Every believer is fully equipped; it is part of the salvation package Jesus gave us. We just need to unpack it and get it back into regular use.

Let's drill down into this unusual term *the eyes of your heart*. Eyes are for observing things. They record the reality of the world around us. Their sole purpose is to deliver information to us about our environment, and from this information we determine our response. Our natural eyes deliver information about the physical world around us; they take in the facts and provide us with the intelligence we need to come up with our best course of action.

Our spiritual eyes (or the eyes of our heart) work in the same way in the spiritual realm. Their purpose is to inform us about the realities of the spiritual environment we are in, so that we can live wisely and well.

Our physical eyes gather information, and our spiritual eyes gather revelation.

Our physical eyes are in our physical body; our spiritual eyes operate at the deeper level of the heart.

Our physical eyes do not have the capacity to observe spiritual truth; they can present to us only a reality based on the evidence on the ground. Our physical eyes cannot see God, they cannot see His kingdom, and they cannot see the spiritual transformation that has occurred in us as a result of the work Jesus undertook on the cross.

Our physical eyes can observe only earthbound evidence. They see only the evidence of Adam's "good and evil" world—it's a mixed bag of success, happiness and plenty, mixed together with brokenness, failure and lack. Our physical eyes deliver to us a newsreel of the ups and downs that make up life on planet earth. They cannot see the realities of God's kingdom, so they hold us in the grip of human endeavour.

As Christians we need the realities of the kingdom of God, yet more often than not we attempt to lay hold of them through the means reported to us by our physical eyes. In so doing, we measure the reality of God's love and favour on the basis of our circumstances. We interpret a spiritual truth on the basis of physical evidence, and we take earthly information and elevate it to superiority over spiritual revelation.

We agree with Adam instead of agreeing with God.

In contrast, revelation is not found in physical circumstances; it is found in the cross of Christ. The cross of Christ is the physical expression of reality as God sees it—God says "Jesus is My truth for you; He is the evidence of your true self, the self I love."

Only revelation has the ability to grasp this—it is above natural information, and it cannot be contained in our well-articulated theologies and doctrines. Revelation takes the task of determining our identity away from our head, and places it into our heart where it belongs.

Don't be scared of the term *revelation*; it is not a fluffy, emotional thing. Rather it is a fact that we know deep in our hearts, which surpasses our intellectual machinations.

Information cannot accomplish the same outcomes as revelation, because it is limited by physical facts and reasoning. Revelation goes where information cannot go; it takes us beyond our physical environment into the wonders of a world that surpasses our wildest imaginings. We need to live in revelation if we are to partake in the extravagance of the kingdom of God.

As I have said, revelation is found only at the foot of the cross.

Revelation exceeds every limitation of the information derived from our physical circumstances, because it is based on a higher truth—the love and life of God, which is ours in Christ. Revelation observes just one thing—I am the object of God's unfailing, unconditional outpouring of love. This love flooded through me when Jesus rescued me from Adam's inheritance and placed me into God, and now I have no identity but the one Jesus gave me. This identity is completely independent of my physical circumstances; I am who God says I am, not Adam.

My worthiness to consider myself this way is not derived from the earthly information about me; if that were so, I would be a wretched failure. It is derived from the expression of God's heart. God spoke a word over me, and that word has a name: *Jesus*. He is God's Word over my life. He is my identity (I no longer live, but Christ lives in me). My true self can surface only when I abandon the world's information about me and embrace the love of God revealed in Jesus—He is my revelation.

Information weakens me. Revelation strengthens me.

In the past I attempted to gain the realities of revelation through the means of information. I attempted to get God to fit into my tidy observations of life. Now I hide myself in His observations about me, and He sees me only in the context of the redemption of Jesus. God does not see my earthly perspective; He sees something so superior that the earthly view is completely eclipsed by it. I am His perfect son, made righteous by the blood of Jesus.

CHAPTER 15

God's View Of Things

The angels are puzzled by some of my earthly antics and responses to God. They too are fully aware of the scale of the accomplishments of the cross, and they wonder when I will see it for myself and choose it as my true and real self.

We must understand that the love of God is the overwhelming fact of the heavenly realm. It obscures and blocks out everything earthly that Adam raised up to compete with it, because the blood of Christ has reset the nature of humanity back to its original settings. There is no truth in heaven but that the blood of Christ has let the love of God loose in us again.

God does not see what we see.

He knows everything, so it follows that He is well informed about our earthly struggles—but this knowledge is so completely overshadowed by our true condition in Christ that it barely causes a ripple in His mind. The reality that God sees over our lives is that we are the product of all the creative urge of His heart expressed in Christ. He will never again see us as corks tossed to and fro by the chaos of life on earth—and He wants us to take a good hard look at the claims made by the blood of Christ and agree with Him too.

Adam wanted God to take a more earthly view of things. He wanted God to agree with him and accept that the value of humanity is the product of our ability to produce good and evil. But if God accepted that, then He would have effectively ceased to be God—He would have become like us, valuing our lifestyle and performance over His unconditional love. That's what satan wanted; he wanted to get God to stop being God so that he could take over the top job. But God remained true to Himself and loved us with an impossible love.

*God wants us to believe in His true nature,
not in the one that satan fabricated for Him.*

This has been satan's agenda all along. Satan knew that if he could get God to be untrue to His real identity, then he could rightly assume the throne. All satan had to do was to get God to participate in Adam's remodelled program by accepting humanity on the basis of their performance instead of His love, and then satan would have had Him. But satan underestimated God and he underestimated God's love. God enacted the plan that He had prepared before time began, and Jesus became the love expression of God. Revelation 13:8 refers to Jesus as *"the lamb that was slain from the creation of the world"*—God's solution for humanity would always be based on His love, a love that has defined him for all eternity, and never on our religious and lifestyle choices.

As history unfolded, the children of Adam relentlessly pursued their quest to change God; religion, sacrifice, ritual and lifestyle all became the canvas upon which humanity painted their virtue in the hope that they could pull God down into their self-oriented world. However, God remained true to Himself and continued to love us for His reason, not ours, because He *is* love. If He had relented and loved us for our reasons, then He would have become like one of us and descended under the dome of man-made worth. He would have become mortal just like Adam did and given up His divine nature.

Religion (including modern religion) wants to continue the quest of Adam—it wants God to elevate the value of our personal best to parity with Jesus. Religion takes the lifestyle of Jesus and turns it into a model for us to mould ourselves to; in doing so, it continues to put before God the ultimatum to "judge us by what we do."

But Jesus didn't come as our example; He came as our substitute. The blood of Jesus calls out to us, not to conform to His example, but to stop trying and simply let His blood do the task for which it was shed—transform us back into sons and daughters of God. If we define ourselves by attempting to copy Jesus' example, then we remain children of Adam; but if we cease from our self-generated labours, we become sons of God. Jesus is certainly the best possible example of a Godly life, but we have no inherent capacity to model it.

> *Through faith in Jesus we become sons of the purest bloodline ever conceived,*
> *we partake in the unadulterated life of God.*

Religion wants to claim a place in God's family tree through its own attributes, but God will not mix our personal sacrifices with the pure blood of Jesus. We either come clothed only in the righteousness of Christ, or not at all.

Can you see this? If God receives our self-made worth and mixes it with the divine bloodline, then the very essence of the divine nature is diluted to human standards. No matter how much we want God to value us on the basis of our good lifestyle, He cannot. By doing so, He would rob us of the thing we most need—to be accepted on the basis of His divine love.

Yet surprisingly, when we embrace this divine love, it empowers us to also lead great lives of love.

The eyes of our heart see the magnificence of God's love and enable us to cast our entire existence into it with no thought for our personal worthiness.

This is the difference between our natural eyes and the eyes of our heart; the eyes of our heart do not see things—they see love. They see a love that is so compelling that we are able to lift ourselves above all the clamouring of the natural realm and rest in the most impossible of all truths: that we are not loved because of what we do, but because of what Christ has done in us.

This is the "good news."

CHAPTER 16
The Cost

Humanity has craved the message of God's unconditional love since they walked out of the garden of God's pleasure all those years ago. Jesus says, *"I am the gate, no one enters but through me,"* and we too enter back in to the pleasure for which we were made simply by believing in Him.

Does it sound too easy?

It is easy in terms of human effort, but it's not easy in terms of personal cost—we must entrust God with our entire identity and sense of worth, which is the exact opposite of human effort.

Don't let this last statement confuse you; this is not yet another formula we adopt to get what we really want. This is not another trumped-up process to get health, prosperity or whatever—this is a declaration to God that *He* is what we really want and that we entrust our entire self, our future, and our eternity into Him and His safekeeping.

So now there is a line in the sand before us all; one side of the line holds me in the insecurities of Adam's legacy (I am the sum total of the good and evil in my life), and the other side releases me to the love and life of God. It sounds easy until we really examine the ramifications of what I am saying; I am suggesting that we never again value ourselves before God by anything that we do. And the flip side is that we always assume upon God's favour and love, naked of any qualification but the blood of Christ.

At this point many will walk away; they will not be able to trust God with their sense of worth to that degree—inadvertently choosing to remain in the safety of Adam's self-made worth. They have lived for too long in self-dependence to embrace such a radical gospel, thinking that it goes too far, and that it lets us off the hook too easily.

Yet that is exactly the point. God has given us a salvation that lets us off the hook without lifting a finger, but we would prefer to depend on ourselves (at least a little bit).

We are more comfortable with the sentiment expressed in the old hymn "I Have Decided to Follow Jesus," which depicts a life of bearing our cross in the footsteps of Jesus until He returns for us. It is certainly a noble and stirring song, but it misses the point; Jesus came to relieve me of my self-sacrificing and release me into a Spirit-energised life. We have for too long thought that God wants us to offer Him a life of self-sacrificed surrender, when He really wants us to simply surrender ourselves into His love.

The first option is all about giving ourselves to God;
the second is about God giving Himself to us.

Anything less than the excellence of God's gift with no strings attached diminishes Him (and us).

In 2 Corinthians 9:15 Pauls calls it *"God's indescribable gift."* It is beyond description with normal earthly superlatives, exceeding even the best of our most lofty notions, and transcending anything we have available in our sense-based information banks. God's gift of love bursts through the dome of human thought that we built to contain Him.

Only the eyes of the heart can truly behold the eminent flawlessness of God's loving nature.

Quite often we send our spiritual eyes on an errand for which they weren't designed. We want God to show us a supernatural display or perhaps a vision of angels; in other words, we want a touch from God. But before any of that can happen, we must desire God for Himself, *not for what He does.*

Ephesians 1:18 puts it so well: *"That you may know the hope...the riches... the glorious power."* We cannot know these things if we have not first discovered the heart behind them. Ephesians 3:19 says, *"And to know this love that surpasses knowledge – that you may be filled to the measure of all the fullness of God."* We must know God's love in a way that surpasses human knowledge (a deep revelation of His love) *so that* we can be filled with the fullness of God.

Our spiritual eyes are designed to grasp just one thing—the extraordinary love of God. From this one revelation overflows every endeavour of the Spirit-energised life. All that we need for life and godliness are the spontaneous overflow of the revelation that we are eternally lost in the great love of our Father God.

If we ask God to simply reveal to us His love, then He will also reveal every other aspect of His vast character. God's love is the doorway into the great heavenly banquet of His favour and blessing. In John 5:20 we read, *"For the Father loves the Son and shows him all he does."* When we gain a revelation of the Father's love, all that the Father does will also be revealed to us.

> *The Christian life is primarily about one thing:*
> *knowing God's love.*

No ministry, no service, no gifting has any relevance without it. 1 Corinthians 13 speaks of all of the spiritual endeavours of humankind and concludes that they are meaningless, just man-made noise, without love. And the same applies to God; He cannot express Himself but by the means of love, so it is imperative that we discover God's love for ourselves.

Jesus could accomplish His earthly mission only because He was energised by His Father's love. Without the revelation that His Father loved Him, He was no different than Adam.

And neither can we ever rise to our true selves without a profound and personal revelation of His love for us—not a cerebral knowledge, but a personal revelation.

It may seem like I am spending too much time banging away at the subject of God's love, but I am doing it for a reason—the most important reason of all. If we do not gain a revelation that God loves us quite apart from what we do, be it ministry (giving out) or selfishness (taking in), then we will always connect His love to our performance on the scales of good and evil.

CHAPTER 17

The God Kind Of Love

God loves me because He must—it is the essence of His nature—and I receive that love because it is the essence of my God-given design to do so. As I receive God's love, my nature conforms to His and so I also love.

> *God loves me irrespective of my response;*
> *if He didn't love me, His nature would be diminished.*
> *And in the same way, my nature is diminished*
> *if I do not choose to allow God's love to saturate my being.*

Religion exhorts us to be loving for God; it compels us to present God with our best so that He can love us, but faith turns this upside down. We have no capacity to really love until we have learned to rest easy in God's love—irrespective of what we have done.

This is how far we have departed from the truth.

We may indeed be capable of great acts of love apart from God, but these acts are merely earth-bound, altruistic endeavours unless the Spirit energises them. Many people live lives of selfless service, but that service counts for nothing in the divine realm if it is self-generated; only the Spirit can energise acts of love that count in the economy of heaven.

In the final analysis, the world doesn't actually need more of my love or your love; it needs to discover God's love. There may be a momentary blessing in an act of love performed by a human being, but that love cannot transform anyone. Only God's love can take the wretchedness of Adam and transform it into the perfection of Christ.

Human love is a good thing; as the saying goes, "it makes the world go 'round." The world craves love like they thirst for water in the desert. But don't make the mistake of thinking that God is looking over the bannisters of heaven hoping that people will change the world by loving each other. We don't possess the "world changing" kind of love within us. The only love that changes the world is the God kind of love, and it cannot operate in us until we have learned to lean back into the certainty of God's unfailing loving nature.

Religion wants to motivate us to great acts of selfless love, but God says, "learn of Me first, and then your love will be energised by Mine."

Jesus changed the world when he expressed the Father's love. He did two things: a physical expression of love that attended to our earthly needs, and a spiritual expression of love that rebuilt our union with His Father. We earthlings have a tendency to relate to God on the basis of our earthly needs more than our spiritual need, yet we are primarily not of the earth; we are spiritual beings just passing through this physical life.

For example, we religiously say grace before every meal, yet we rarely express our gratitude for the staggering gift of eternal life. The gift of spiritual life is by far the most extravagant expression of God's heart, yet we focus our attention on the much smaller finite realities.

It is the dome problem all over again. We don't tangibly perceive that we are partaking of God's divine life, so we relegate it to lesser value. In reality, it is of infinitely more value than our earthly life; we just haven't seen it like that since Adam's mutiny.

Jesus came so that the dome over us would be lifted off and we would at last see the scale of God's lavish love—He came to remove the legacy of Adam and let the life of God back in. Jesus didn't come to re-energise the legacy of Adam by setting us the impossible task of copying His example; He came to deflate Adam's dome and fill us with His divine life again… then we can actually do the impossible just as He (Jesus) did.

For most of us, this requires a quantum shift in our thinking. Our worth has been defined for so long by our earthly performance that it's hard to liberate ourselves from our old mindset and embrace the crazy notion that God loves us because of who He is, and not because of who we are.

It's like gum boots stuck in thick mud; it takes all of our energy to get free—such is the pull of Adam's legacy. But we must pull ourselves free of this debilitating thinking, lest we spend our remaining days on earth attempting to be something God doesn't even want us to be.

God wants us to fly over the vagaries of life on earth knowing that our identity and security is firmly established in His love, not in our attempts to overcome our earthly limitations.

> *He made us to be carried aloft by His Spirit.*
> *That is our true identity.*

Toughing it out without the benefit of having the Holy Spirit bear the load is the foolishness of religion. God desires and intends that we unburden ourselves, not set ourselves up as self-appointed martyrs.

It seems to come with the turf, however. Religion always seems to try to extract self-sacrifice, but there is no sacrifice left for us to make when we rest in Christ's sacrifice. Hardship that results as an outcome of our Christian walk cannot be compared to the riches of living in God's love; He carries the burden, not us. If the Christian life seems hard and burdensome, then I would suggest it's time to re-evaluate and possibly start over. It's never too late to discover the joy of living in the lightness of God's love.

Life tends to paint us into a corner; options that we may have seriously considered when we were younger don't seem as viable as the years roll by. Our reluctance causes us to step back from the self-awareness line for fear of making a big mistake, and in so doing we pull the very dome that Christ has lifted off back down over ourselves. *If you are younger, I encourage you to cast caution to the wind and just do it.*

> *We must step across the line—*
> *embracing God's extravagant love*
> *is the most Christian thing we can do.*

CHAPTER 18

The Better Way

God is not cheering from the sidelines, hoping we can hold the line, as we grit our teeth and bear up under the pressure. Quite the contrary, He says, *"My yoke is easy and my burden is light."* If we are being crushed by life, then it's reasonable to assume that there has to be a better way.

The better way is the way we (humanity) were designed, to be back in the garden of God's pleasure.

To get our heads around this alternative way we need to venture back in time to the beginning, and then follow the progressive outcomes of Adam's "mad adventure into self-realisation."

For the greater part of my life I had perceived the story of human history from the perspective of one living under the dome of our self-obsessed thinking. I thought that was all there was, because it was all I could see. The greater reality of God's love and life was a theology rather than a reality—like Truman, I had an inkling there was more out there, but I didn't know how to make it real.

This is how it all started.

Adam and Eve lived with God in a seamless overlapping of the spiritual and natural realms. There was no separation between these realms; they were in fact one perfectly blended reality. Adam and Eve did not consciously connect with God as physical beings; they didn't need to, because their spirit was in perfect union with God. God made them that way—they were "born of God."

All through the New Testament we read about this union as the outcome of the work of Christ on the cross. Galatians 2:20 *"I no longer live, but Christ lives in me."* Colossians 1:27 *"The mystery which is Christ in you."* John 14:28 *"On that day you will realize that I am in my Father, and you are in me, and I am in you."*

These Scriptures are not referring to a new idea that Jesus came up with at the time of His resurrection; they are referring to the original idea that His Father came up with when He created the world. Humanity was originally designed for this union; it is the hallmark of our existence.

The reality of these two blended realms is very difficult for us to grasp; our self-based existence effectively eclipses the spiritual realm from view, and so we have no way to conceptualise the original model.

But that is what we are attempting to do in these pages—lay hold of a reality that has been lost to humanity for most of its history. It was restored to us when Jesus was resurrected. At that time, he reactivated the eyes of our heart—but religion has effectively kept that reality from us ever since.

A short diversion: religion maintains the eyes of humanity on itself. It perpetuates the problem because it refuses to embrace the notion that God loves us because of who He is, not because of what we do.

The original model of human existence is best understood through the example of Jesus in the Gospel of John. This book has provided us with a unique perspective as it describes the life of one living without the dome of self-consciousness. The Gospel of John unfolds the reality of living without the separation of realms. Jesus did it naturally; He knew no other way to be—and John records it for our enlightenment.

The other gospels record history from the observation of events in the theatre of life in and around the Holy Land at that time, but John records the life of Jesus seamlessly living in two realms at once.

We have much to learn from the Gospel of John.

In John's gospel we hear such statements as, *"the Son can do nothing without the Father"* and *"the Father loves the Son and shows him all that he does"* and even *"if you have seen me, you have seen the Father."* Jesus' short sojourn in the flesh was not a withdrawal from His Father's realm; He was equally aware of His Father's presence both in the spirit and in the flesh. The addition of the flesh to Jesus' existence did not diminish the reality of His Father to Him.

This blended reality is the same reality that Adam enjoyed in the beginning. In fact in 1 Corinthians 15:45, Paul refers to Jesus as *"the last Adam."* In the beginning Adam was completely aware of the Father's presence all around him and even in him; it was the stuff of his daily life. God was the whole truth of his existence, and there was no reality that did not have the presence of God filling it.

The dome of our self-consciousness has added separation; it has caused us to perceive an existence for humanity where the physical and the spiritual come together from time to time, or interact independently and then connectedly, as the need arises. This was not Adam's experience in the beginning, and it was not Jesus' experience until He lifted the dome off humanity and carried it in His own body into the grave. Jesus experienced separation from His Father only when He took on the fallen nature of humanity and cried out, *"My God, My God, why have you forsaken me?"* Even then, His Father remained present; however with the addition of the eyes of the flesh as He carried our fallen nature into the grave, the Father's presence was hidden from Jesus view.

Jesus took the spiritual blindness of humanity into the grave;
He killed it for all eternity so that we can see His Father once again
as the great lover of our souls.

Satan tempted Adam and Eve with a new reality. He offered them the ability to perceive life from the perspective of good and evil, a life that would elevate self to supremacy, a life that would open up to them a god-like status as creators and keepers of their self-oriented world. They already had the natural realm in which to base this new world order (God had given it to them), and so they carved off the physical realm from the spiritual realm, and established it as their own kingdom.

CHAPTER 19
The Natural Realm

Inside Adam's new kingdom, things were different; God was not invited unless He accepted humanity on their own terms. Adam and Eve chose good and evil as the currency of this new kingdom. It would purchase every commodity necessary, from personal happiness to the presence of God.

I referred much earlier in this book to the changes experienced by Adam and Eve as a result of their "independence day." They observed their nakedness for the first time as the measure of their personal worth. We also read a few verses later that God came looking for them in the cool of the day—this was a post-independence phenomenon, for the first time ever God had to seek them out in the natural realm. They were no longer able to perceive God in His own realm.

Like all of the theology I developed under the dome, I had always assumed that God and Adam met for an evening stroll every day to chat about the day's activities and update each other about their respective realms, but now I see this meeting in the cool of the day was a once-off event—God had to go looking for Adam and Eve because they had taken to hiding in the physical realm.

Ever-presence was replaced by occasional physical proximity—this was not an upgrade.

The ultimate outcome of this independence was that God had to post an angelic guard at the gateway to the Garden of Eden so that Adam could not wander over to the Tree of Life and partake of God's life as the whim took him. If Adam did that, he would have lived forever within the fallen nature as one contained for all eternity under the dome of human effort.

The self-focused fallen nature is so debilitating to our original design that God could not allow Adam and Eve to carry it over into eternity.

What follows in the pages of the Old Testament is a litany of the self-man at work. Page after page records a tragedy of epic proportions unfolding before our eyes like a train wreck, as the self-made man's attempts to construct a life of value out of his independence from the only true source of life. This record of human history is nothing short of disastrous.

Once again I attempted to apply my under-the-dome theology to understand what was going on in those recorded events, but I was always limited by my view that God was in charge. Yet God wasn't in charge of Adam's choice to be independent, and consequently He wasn't in charge of the calamitous outcomes that resulted.

By choosing to set up his world to operate by good and evil, Adam had placed before God a system that was foreign to the divine way; so, in reality, Adam and his descendants were in charge... not God.

This was the ultimate attempt to re-make the nature of God.

Fast forward to Moses: we are presented with scenes of violence and a rigid system of law and religion that seems quite out of sync with a loving God—yet all seemingly at God's direct command. You could be forgiven for thinking that God has a split personality—harsh, yet loving; violent, yet peaceful.

All of this violence and legalism can be properly understood only when it is viewed from the fact that Adam had created a new world order based on good and evil. This new world order extended its influence to everyone, *even God!*

Does that sound like too much of a stretch? Does is sound preposterous that the almighty, sovereign God could be subject to the petty influences of His created beings? Don't get me wrong—I am not suggesting that Adam changed God. But I am suggesting that God's ability to operate according to His heart's desire in regard to the natural realm was severely restricted by Adam's choice. Such is the regard that God has for our independent will, that He will not oppose it when we insist on our right to dominion.

The scenario Adam presented to God was this: I still want to be in relationship with You, I still want Your favour and blessing in my life, and I still want You to hold the earth and all that is in it together as You always have—but now You will have to do it within the limitations of good and evil, and not your spontaneous expression of unconditional love.

No wonder God had to shut the gate to Paradise. If this sort of thinking had been allowed to roam free in the halls of heaven, it would have changed humanity's eternity for the worst, *forever.*

God could have destroyed the whole thing and started again. How amazing that He didn't. Instead He set about redeeming His creation…from itself.

On the one hand, God held his fallen creation in place by overseeing good and evil with the necessary religious and legal system needed to control it; and on the other hand, He set in train a redemption for humanity that would return it to the original model.

This is the ultimate gesture of God's love. Not only did He respect Adam's desire to control the world, but He also prepared a solution for humanity that would give us a second chance to know God according to our original design. God wasn't in the violence, religion and legalism; this was all initiated by Adam's choice. And God continued to love us all until our salvation was in place.

I have to confess that all I have written above was not the way I saw things for most of my Christian life. I thought that God was behind it all, that He had a big investment in religion and violence, and that getting people to do the right thing was His highest objective. But I see now that God wasn't in it at all. Religion exists only because Adam required a religious system that would mesh with good and evil.

I know this now because the Bible makes it clear in Scriptures like Hebrews chapter eight, which refer to God's dissatisfaction with religion and the law and His intention to enact a far better way through the cross of Jesus.

But it took me a long time to make the leap from the notion that religion somehow reflected God's heart, to my new understanding that He hates religion as much as I do.

Another Scripture that has helped is Mark 2:27—*"Then Jesus told them, The Sabbath was made for man, not man for the Sabbath."* The point of this Scripture is that we were not made by God to fit into a religious system—the religious system was made only because man insisted on the way of good and evil. And if the Sabbath was given in response to man's need for a system to contain good and evil, then it follows that all of the cultural and lifestyle requirements of religion are also initiated by man not God.

Don't make the mistake of thinking of religion as the same as church involvement. The two may actually take place together, but that is not what God had in mind. We are the body of Christ who are also sometimes called the church; we have free and full access to the heart of God without the performance of any ritual, membership or system. We have this access on the basis of our faith in Jesus and *that is all*—no activity or affiliation qualifies or disqualifies us, only faith gives us entrance. We are carried into God's presence by the blood of Jesus alone.

I am not diminishing the value of churches and Christian communities of all kinds; in fact, I believe they are very often a wonderful environment for living out our faith with like-minded believers. But we must know where to go to get what. Only faith in the work Jesus completed on the cross can transport us from death to life.

So what is the point of religion?

There is no point at all. We do not need a religious system to present us holy before the Father's presence—only faith in Jesus can do that. We do not need any activity, meeting or environment to have the full flood of God's love flowing through our lives. All we need to do is look to Jesus and ask Him to take us home with Him to meet His Father, and it is done.

> ***Religion keeps a process going for a lifetime***
> ***which faith accomplished in the blink of an eye.***

Should we go to church?

There is no "should" in God's heart. All of the "shoulds" have been satisfied in Christ. But now we can choose to go to church or any other activity that overflows from the love of God with freedom, boldness and confidence.

The main thing is that we shake off the notion that God is watching our lives on the lookout for a slipup or failure. God is completely happy with us because He sees the virtue of Jesus coursing through our being; our only part is to keep our eyes fixed on Jesus (not Adam).

CHAPTER 20

The Kingdom Of God

As we allow ourselves to revel in the unconditional love of God, a wonderful new thing takes place—the separation between us and God dissolves, and we find ourselves living in two realms seamlessly. The kingdom of the earth is melded with the kingdom of heaven, and time and eternity are joined into one perfect reality again, with God through all and in all.

At this point the work that Jesus came to do has been satisfied, all that He came to accomplish is done and we are at home where we belong. *"Very truly I tell you, whoever hears my word and believes him who sent me <u>has</u> eternal life and will not be judged but <u>has</u> crossed over from death to life"* (John 5:24).

What a remarkable thing to think that all Jesus intended for me when He carried my lost nature onto the cross in His crucifixion is now accomplished. He has no more up His sleeve. I am in possession of the kingdom of God. He has held nothing back. As surely as Jesus died and rose again, so also did I, and now I live out every remaining moment of my life in the completeness of His nature.

There is no more; I have it all.

I will have no more when I die and depart this earthly life than I have right now. The kingdom of God is mine; there is no more than that. And while I remain here, I embark on the adventure of discovering how to live as one who is in possession of God's best.

The dome has been lifted off me; there is no longer any separation between God and me. He is in me, and I am in Him, and I am beginning to see Him as He truly is.

I feel a bit like Adam may have felt when he first opened his eyes and found himself saturated in the glorious love of God. I'm new at this, but unlike Adam, I have a lot of built-up thinking to clear away so that I can walk in my true reality. That's okay—God's got me, and that's the main thing. The living out of it all will flow as I become accustomed to my new world.

The echo of Adam's thinking continues to replay in my mind. The only thing I can do about that is to deliberately choose to live in God's love. I will make mistakes along the way, but that can't disqualify me. I have stepped over the line, and my old self-conscious world is slowly disappearing in the rearview mirror.

My ability to live boldly and freely in this new world is not the measure of its reality; it is real because God says so, and I believe Him. The eyes of my heart are slowly opening, but they have many years of misuse to overcome. The main thing is that I have made the choice to open them and see my true identity and reality once again.

I would like to engage with my new reality in spontaneous confidence. I would like to see all of the outcomes of the cross materialising in my life now—but it takes time for faith to grow, so I simply keep putting one foot in front of the other, walking this out with the assurance that God is beside me, knowing that He is fully engaged even if my new thinking is not yet as fully engaged as I would like.

I John 3:2 puts it so well: *"Dear friends, now we are children of God, and what we will be has not yet been made known. But we know that when Christ appears, we shall be like him."* It seems to me that the more I see Him and the more His true nature appears before me, the more I will be transformed into His likeness. Then the physical realm and the spiritual realm will have become perfectly reunited to me, and I will live as Jesus did on earth... just as He said I would.

I am already living in eternity—John 5:24 tells me so—and I will see the reality of this more clearly as the completeness of His work on the cross comes more and more into focus.

One day I will die and the veil of the natural realm will fall away. Then I will see clearly what I have had all along. I will know then that I was complete in Christ the whole time, He had accomplished the task He was sent to do, and the only thing lacking in me was my ability to see it with clarity.

Perhaps the greatest discovery I have made since my spiritual eyes have begun to take in the magnificence of God's love again is that God Himself is the prize. For most of my life, I thought God was the means by which we obtain the prize—health, prosperity, relationships, going to heaven, etc. But it has come as such a surprise to discover that it is all about Him, and if I have Him, then I have everything I need.

That's not just another way to get my hands on the earthly things I really want. It's that I am discovering that all I really need in life is to be hidden in God's love. The things of the earth that seemed to demand my attention are growing strangely dim as I discover the magnitude of my heavenly Father's heart.

It's like I was made for this; it fills me like nothing else.

But this is where I feel most like I am swimming against the stream. I have spent so long in Christian circles that promote the "name it and claim it" message that I feel like a lone voice at times. To suggest that God wants to give us Himself—not houses, cars, and success—is a serious departure from the mainstream ultra-grace message. Not that I think God doesn't want us to have these things; it's just that, in themselves, they have a tendency to keep us under Adam's dome, fixing our gaze on the stuff of the natural realm instead of on Jesus.

It's a kind of divine dare.

I dare you to believe in My love for you so much that you swing your gaze away from things, and onto Me. I dare you to want to lean back into My love for you so much that you would choose it over success and material or physical well-being.

If you could truly see My love for you as it really is, you would lose yourself in the sublime wonder of it in a heartbeat. But you don't, because you can't see it. And the reason you can't see it is because you don't really understand what the cross of Jesus was all about.

CHAPTER 21

The Sin Problem

It's easy to slip into the thinking that it was all about me—my sin, my need for forgiveness—but it is bigger than that. It is about the restoration of my original design; it is about love, perfection, holiness and glory. Jesus didn't come to simply provide me with a pardon for my sins; He came to restore me to the reality that defined me when He first created human life. Pardoning my sins resolves my physical self; it deals with the stuff that has been produced by my flesh. But the real and most profound outcome of Jesus' sacrifice is that I have been reunited back into the seamless union with God that was broken by Adam's independence. God once again defines me, and His love, perfection, holiness, and glory are now my defining characteristics too.

If you think the cross was only about forgiveness and not about reunion, then you have been missing out on the best part.

Forgiveness indeed resolves our guilty status, but more than that, it also gives us the right to live as sons and daughters of God. Stepping into our rightful, God-given identity is up to us.

Our difficulty is that we carry over the echo of our past guilt into our new identity in Christ. We have been defined by guilt for so long, and are so aware that we continue to fall short of the mark, that we find it hard to assume the reality of our true selves.

While we continue to feel unworthy, we will never embrace the true identity that Jesus gave us. The Bible is clear that we have been made new creations, yet we often relegate this truth into subjection to the earthly evidence. We place the Word of God into subjection to the word of Adam.

This is not what the cross of Jesus is all about!

The cross of Jesus is about re-elevating the truth as God sees it to superiority over the evidence on the ground. It is about believing in an invisible fact over that which is more visibly evident in our daily lives, and it is about declaring ourselves to be the righteousness of God when the world around us thinks we are failures, unfit for any esteem—least of all to be the very objects of God's love.

If we are not prepared to elevate ourselves to the lofty status that the cross of Jesus has provided for us, then we are choosing an inferior identity and settling for meagre handouts that satisfy only our earthly needs. There is no lasting joy in new houses and cars, and besides they need to be frequently upgraded to keep up with the pack. Only God Himself can satisfy the deepest yearning of our hearts.

Jesus covers this issue in Matthew 6:25-33 where He speaks about worry. First, He speaks of the birds of the air, then the lilies of the field, and then He goes on to explain that God looks after them even though they are of much less value than we are. He concludes with these words: *"So do not worry, saying, 'What shall we eat?' or 'What shall we drink?' or 'What shall we wear?' For the pagans run after these things, and your heavenly Father knows that you need them. But seek first his kingdom and his righteousness, and all these things will be given to you as well."*

From under the dome it seems like Jesus is saying, "If you work hard in my kingdom, and live righteously, then I will reward you by giving you what you need." But once the dome is lifted away, we see that He is actually saying, "When you gain a revelation of the true nature of my kingdom and embrace my freely given love and righteousness, then all you need on earth will overflow from your identity as God's beloved."

These are two entirely different scenarios. The first promotes the efforts of man to influence the charity of God. The second assumes upon the love of God without the addition of any human effort. The first is motivated by the self-made currency of humanity that has trading power under the dome; the second is motivated by the precious blood of Jesus, which is the currency of heaven.

My old thinking—that God wanted me to present Him with my best before He could respond with His best—is long gone. Now I am settling into life in His kingdom, I am getting used to my new righteous identity, and I rest in quiet confidence as I wait for all my earthly needs to be given to me as well.

CHAPTER 22
Faith

It's taken a while, but I am finally adjusting to the fact that He will never leave me nor forsake me—and this 'resting in His love' is the same faith that Jesus spoke of so often.

By embracing my new identity in Christ, I am agreeing with God's opinion of me—and that's what faith is—seeing things how God sees them and agreeing with Him. When we see the love of God in and over us, every obstacle to God's lavish provision is removed—*that* is faith.

> *It is impossible to have true faith*
> *without being obsessed with the love of God.*

Faith is not generated by self-effort; it is living in an environment saturated in God's true nature.

It's just like Jesus sleeping in the boat while the storm raged all around; He was more in His Father's love, than He was in the boat. The disciples were fearful and panicked, thinking they might drown; but Jesus said, "Where is your faith?" Their faith was more in the storm's capacity to do them harm, than in their Father's capacity to keep them safe. They couldn't see the Father's love; they could only see the storm, so they put their faith in the thing they could see most clearly.

As we learn to rest in the environment of God's love, we find ourselves asking less and less of God because we know deep down that He gave us everything He owns when He gave up His Son's life for us. Worry falls away, because there is nothing to worry about as we take our place around the banquet of God's love. Fear is a thing of the past, because nothing can separate us from the love of God.

This is the way we were designed to live in the beginning; we were designed to rest with absolute confidence that nothing can separate us from God's love. It is not wishful thinking or desperate hoping. It is instead restfully easing back into the love of God, and it begins when we make the radical leap of deciding that God can be trusted *with everything.*

Most Christians I know (myself included) have spent most of our lives not entrusting ourselves into God's love. We might have said the words. We might even have repeated the catch cries of Christianity. But that is not the same as looking Jesus in the eye and declaring, "From this moment forward, I entrust every fibre of my being into the safety of your love. I hold nothing back. I have no fallback position. You are now the source of my life.

"I am burning the bridge of Adam's self-reliance behind me; there is no way back to the old way. I have examined Your love for me and determined that it is enough, more than enough, and from this moment forward I surrender myself over to Your love.

"I could not do this were it not for the cross. The cross has shown me the value I hold in Your heart, and so I abandon all of my reservations to the truth that was expressed when You died for me.

"The cross of Christ does not represent a religion. I do not take it as an emblem of my belief system. Rather, it is the death of my old self-sufficient nature, which I gladly walk away from to embrace the security of Your unconditional love."

Arriving at the certainty of this decision is not a flippant thing; it is not a matter of being swept along by the enthusiasm of the crowd. Quite the contrary, it is a lonely and deeply personal thing. First, I consider the love that was expressed on the cross for me as if I were the sole recipient of it, and then I must decide whether I am sufficiently convinced in that love to abandon my entire self into it.

I must decide; only I can do it.

If I do it as a response to the crowd, then I must go back and start over. I can make this decision only if I am uniquely and individually moved by the love of God. I must do it for one reason only—because I am convinced that He died for me, and I believe that the only life worth having is to abandon myself to His love. Serving or ministering or giving back has not even entered my head at this point. I am making this decision for one reason only, a reason much higher than any personal response I might make—because I believe in His love for me and cannot live without it as the source of my existence.

Then, in an instant, I am born again, born of God.

No longer am I like the majority of earthlings who depend upon themselves. I am now an alien unlike the other inhabitants of the planet. My life source is from elsewhere, from a completely different realm, and my being is sustained by the love of God. Good and evil are not my currency; self-effort does not provide for me. My provision comes directly from the unconditional love of God.

> *He said that He loves me;*
> *He said He will never leave me,*
> *and that has become the overriding fact of my life.*

This is not intended to sound super-spiritual or unrealistic; I don't want it to come across that way. I still get up and do a day's work like everyone else. I still live as a responsible citizen of planet earth. But it is the source of my security that has changed—I am learning to rest in the knowledge that God has got me. The words of Hebrews 13:6 ring true: *"So we say with confidence, The Lord is my helper; I will not be afraid. What can man do to me."*

I'm not even suggesting that I won't have difficulties anymore; I expect they will continue to arrive from the failed experiment of good and evil as they always have. But I can't be hurt by them in the same way, because I have relocated my security to God's love.

CHAPTER 23

Beyond Theology

Many will agree with me and give their nod of approval to what I am saying. They will accept the theology of it, but this is more than theology; it is taking a step beyond theology into absolute confidence in an invisible yet life-changing love.

You see, love is more than theology.

Love is not a subject for our consideration and cerebral acceptance. It is a person who knocks on our heart's door and asks our permission to take the place of theology. When we have yielded our existence to the love of God, theology becomes much less relevant; it is no longer required because the subject matter has now become the primary fact of our life—revelation has replaced information.

We do not need to analyse the reality of the air we breathe for it to sustain our earthly bodies, and we do not need to labour with theology to be sustained by the life and love of God—it is simply the fact of our existence.

There is no theology in heaven,
just the radiant presence of God—
and we are now citizens of heaven.

Please don't mistake me. I honour and value good teaching and academic study, but these are of no real value if they are an end in themselves. We must each individually decide if God can be trusted with our existence. It is a decision of the heart not the head, because the head looks for its evidence in the physical realm.

So we are back where Adam began, considering whether to rest in God's love as the source of our existence, or whether to count on our own management of good and evil.

Adam chose himself; he chose to count on his flesh to provide life.

Each of us is confronted with the same decision as Adam. Each of us has the same opportunity to decide on our life source. It is as though each of us is standing in the garden of God between the two trees, and no one can force us to choose; it is up to us.

Jesus said to the Pharisees, *"You won't come to Me to have life,"* and He puts the same question to us: *"Will you come to me to have life?"* He has destroyed the lie of our self-dependence. It was crucified and buried with Him, and now He beckons us to come and have life. He doesn't beckon us to join a religious institution; he beckons us to come to Him to have life. Then our involvement in church makes sense.

There is no denomination or church that has the special privilege of a group pass—only Jesus offers us life, and if we do not personally come to Him to receive it, then we are merely participating in religion.

Who can come?

How difficult is the process?

It is important that we do not approach this question in the same way Adam did. This is not primarily about the physical realm or about self-fulfilment; it is about whether we choose our self-made worth or God's love as the source of our being.

Anyone can come—there is no process!

It is not a process; it is a decision. The only proviso is that we do not come as Adam; only those who exercise their right to be sons and daughters of God can come.

This is the tragedy of much of modern-day Christianity's thinking; people are exhorted to approach God using Adam's method. We are told to present God with our religious and lifestyle best, as if God has changed His mind and decided to accept the flesh on its own terms after all. It's not that God doesn't want us, but rather that our flesh cannot produce righteousness; and only the truly righteous can fellowship with the Most Holy God.

Those who attempt to present God with their religious and lifestyle best to gain access to His kingdom will find themselves confronted with the angelic guard who blocked Adam's way back to the Tree of Life. We cannot partake of the life of God as the sons of Adam.

It would be like working all day in a pigsty, and then bringing our stinking clothing to the foot of the cross and asking Jesus to add it to His sacrifice. The works of the flesh are an offence to the sacrifice of Christ; the only work God requires is that we believe. Jesus made it clear in John 6:28-29: *"'Then the people asked him, what must we do to do the works that God requires?' Jesus answered; the work of God is this, to believe in the one he has sent."*

To present God with our personal best in the hope of gaining His favour is more than simply errant theology, it is an offence to the heart of God; and it is keeping Christians the world over from the reality of their union with God.

These are strong words, yet not unlike the words Paul used in Galatians 3:1-2, *"You foolish Galatians...Are you so foolish? After beginning with the Spirit, are you now trying to attain your goal by human effort?"* In Paul's day, they wanted to add circumcision to the work of Christ; in our day, we are told to add our own modern-day religious responsibilities.

We must grow so confident in the sacrifice of Jesus that we dare to clothe ourselves with His virtue alone as we approach the throne of God.

Even the sacred cow of tithing holds no sway over the heart of God. We assume upon God's love because we are His sons and daughters, not because we satisfy a religious principle. I know of churches that devote fifteen minutes each Sunday to the subject of tithing in an attempt to open the congregation's purse strings. If only a revelation of the unconditional love of God was presented instead! That is the only thing that can release us into a life of abundance.

Jesus is the end of the law—even tithing.

Jesus is the end of the law—not so that we can lead reckless and irresponsible lives, but so that we can be transformed into people who are led by the Spirit.

I would even go so far as to say that God does not want us to satisfy the law. While we are law-conscious, we cannot be Spirit-conscious. The Spirit is much better at training us in righteousness than the law ever was; the Spirit transforms us from the inside, whereas the law is a list of external rules to be outwardly satisfied. God wants us to walk in the Spirit. When we do that, then we will not satisfy the desires of the flesh.

Can you see it?

The law is the way of those who are independent of God; the Spirit is the way of those who are in union with God. The law makes us sin-conscious; the Spirit makes us righteousness-conscious. We were designed by God to be Spirit-led; Adam remade us to be led by the law, and Jesus returned us to our original design.

Remember Paul's statement in 1 Corinthians 6:12? *"Everything is permissible for me."* He was describing the freedom of the Spirit. Then he goes on to say, *"but not everything is beneficial."* He was clarifying that the Spirit doesn't lead us recklessly. Paul was above the law; he lived by the far superior way. He lived as a man energized by the Spirit of God.

Satan fed Adam the lie of self-made worth, Adam believed him, and the dome of the law of good and evil has been the atmosphere of human existence ever since.

And now Jesus calls us back to our true selves.

If we choose to live under the direction of the law, then we remain in the same limited condition as Adam. We are effectively saying to the Holy Spirit, "I'm okay. I have this under control, and I don't need Your help, thanks." This thinking holds us in a dome-like existence; the kingdom of God has been provided to us to occupy and enjoy, but instead we remain inhabitants of our own self-made Seahaven Island.

CHAPTER 24

Empty

In this day and age most Christians acknowledge that the religious system of the nation of Israel with all its sacrifices, holy days and laws is a thing of the past. We don't identify with the practices of that time or engage in them to maintain our relationship with God. Instead we have adopted a different, more modern system. Our system has within it all of the ingredients of the old way, only they have been repackaged and renamed to align with our twenty-first-century context; but it still remains a system based on human merit just like the old one. We still approach God on the basis of our religious and lifestyle practices; we still present ourselves to God on the merits of our personal best.

We don't know how to approach God without the scaffolding of church attendance, Bible reading, worship music and multi-media teaching. We clothe ourselves in the garb of religion just like the children of Israel did, but we don't think of it that way because everyone is doing it; and we don't know what else to do. So we redouble our efforts; we have longer quiet times and pray more and louder in the hope that it will make us feel closer to God and provide the breakthrough.

To base our relationship with God on feelings is Adam's way; it is exalting our flesh to the task that only our spirit can manage—the task of conveying to us our sense of well-being with God.

We have lost the knack of going to God with nothing.

We can't imagine the life Adam and Eve had at the very beginning. They didn't need a system that they would "put on" to approach God. They went to Him naked of self-made virtue, clothed only in His unconditional love. They would never think of approaching God on the merits of their personal best; they were too secure in His lavish, fatherly acceptance of them to do that. It would have been a ridiculous insult to God's love to even consider it.

Yet, on Independence Day everything changed—they became self-conscious.

No matter how sophisticated, well-intentioned or sincere we are when packaging up our response to God, there is only one gateway into His presence; and His name is Jesus. We need to strip it all back, take off our religious securities and come to God clothed in the sacrifice of Christ alone.

To do that we need a fresh understanding of the cross of Christ—we cannot strip off the covering of religion if we are not convinced that the covering of Christ is better. We have become so accustomed to adding Christ to our long list of religious stuff, but the truth of the matter is that He is not just another part of this great big thing we call Christianity—He is the whole of it.

God doesn't care if we celebrate the Passover, drive nails through our hands, or lay prostrate on the floor in worship. He just wants us to rest in His love expressed by Jesus on the cross.

We are too insecure to come to God with nothing.

Can you see it?

Humanity has pulled a covering down over itself. It is the covering of our self-made identity, and now we don't know how to be with God without it.

The good news is that we don't need it anymore (in fact, we never did). Jesus has lifted off our false sense of security and clothed us in the best of all garments—the perfect nature of God.

CHAPTER 25

My Movie

Imagine your life as a movie (just like Truman's) that is played out before your own eyes. You have the lead role, and the movie is a record of all you do; every action, word and emotion is filmed just as it happens in real time. Your life is recorded in every detail. The circumstances and events of your life roll along in a continuous newsreel, your reactions and their consequences interplaying with the wider events to form a story of epic proportions. This is not the story of human history—it is the story of your history, and human history is the theatre where it is played out. From birth to death, the story slowly unfolds complete with all of the joys and disappointments, successes and disasters of your life, and in the end it is over and the cameras shut down.

This movie of your life is a record of how the events happening around you affected you, and about how you responded to them to improve or harm your future. Good and evil occurred all around you, and you made the most (or worst) of it by your decisions and actions. Sometimes you affected things for the better, and sometimes they deteriorated in spite of you. Cause and effect defined your existence, and every new day called upon you to respond as best you could all over again. As a Christian you made choices to manage the ups and downs of life by engaging in good principles and habits, and to some extent these practices kept the worst of life at bay as you crafted the best you could from what was handed to you.

It was all about good management. The most you could hope for was that your best efforts would be enough and life would turn out okay. Fortunately, as a Christian, you had an advantage; good living and careful attention to godly principles like church attendance, prayer and Bible reading would most likely yield a good return, and life would be happy and fruitful.

In the end, God and others will view the movie of your life and decide if it was worth much. You did the best you could, and now it's for others to determine if it was enough. You lived your life, and all of the good and evil has been played out. Maybe God will score you high enough…and maybe He won't. Who knows?

But, what if this is not how God observes your life? What if He sees a completely different reality?

There is a reality that overshadows us so completely that it all but eclipses the earthly drama of our daily lives. That reality is the indwelling presence of the Spirit of Jesus. Jesus explained this in so many ways to His disciples, but none more poignantly than when He told His disciples that they were "already clean." This is the reality that the Father sees, and it is so overwhelmingly true that our earthly issues are nothing more than background noise by comparison.

We want God to be as obsessed with our day-to-day comings and goings as we are, but the fact is that those concerns pale into insignificance compared to the surpassing greatness of our eternal union with Him. Paul had learned to be content in all things—not that He enjoyed his physical struggles, but that the reality of his union with Jesus was so profoundly true to him that it effectively obscured his earthly troubles from view.

I'm not at all suggesting that God doesn't care; I am suggesting that He cares for us so much that He has already placed us into eternity, even before we die. John 5:24 says, *"I tell you the truth, whoever hears my word and believes him who sent me has eternal life and will not be condemned; he has crossed over from death to life."*

The movie that God delights to see is the newsreel of our eternal union with Him through Christ. We have already crossed over from death to life.

And the reality that God sees is the reality we must see.

You might be thinking, "What then of all my daily concerns—my sick child, my financial pressure, my wayward friend? What happens to these? They don't cease to be real just because I shift my focus to Jesus."

Paul had a perspective that, in my observation, is rare today. *"I consider that our present sufferings are not comparable to the glory that will be revealed in us. The creation waits in eager expectation for the revelation of the sons of God"* (Romans 8:18-19).

These verses evidence a sense of order that is not found in today's "name it and claim it" prosperity teaching. Paul is not telling us to petition God endlessly with our list of needs; he is telling us to lift our eyes to the incomparable glory that is ours in Christ. Notice, it's not the glory that will be ours, but that is already ours because we have already crossed over from death to life…only then will we be revealed to all of creation as the sons and daughters of God.

Let me add a further disclaimer; I am not suggesting God wants us to have a spartan life of poverty and suffering, rather I am suggesting that there is a reality that is so superior to our earthly circumstances that it outshines our troubles, and ultimately resolves them, as we learn to rest in our divine union with God.

When we fix our eyes on Jesus, the troubles of the world are seen in a new perspective.

Most of us think we need things and remedies and solutions. We don't even want to contemplate an alternative because we fear it will leave us with less than we need. We want earthly comfort and security, and we can't imagine that the reality of Christ within could possibly be any better earthly things. Yet that is the gospel; Jesus is so much more than the best of earthly things. King David of old yearned for the courts of the Lord, and we too can never be deeply satisfied by anything less that the indwelling Christ.

> ***Jesus didn't primarily come to give us His gifts;***
> ***He came to give us Himself.***

We must discover the value and scale of that statement.

Adam reduced our existence to the shallow fulfilment of earthly life, and we perpetuate his tyranny when we elevate the realm of the flesh above the realm of the Spirit. Jesus Himself said in John 6:63, *"The Spirit gives life, the flesh counts for nothing."* We were made for God, and remade for Him a second time through Christ. Dare we abandon the earth's pull on our hearts and embrace the kingdom of His love?

And guess what? When we do… all things will be added to us as well.

The dome that contains humanity vanishes from sight when we dare to entrust ourselves to God's love as our sole obsession and source. Everything else overflows from that truth and everything else is satisfied by that truth.

Earthly needs are satisfied as we rest in the assurance that our Father loves us. The Father wants our earthly needs satisfied as much as we do, He just wants us learn to trust His love.

The movie of our lives that our Heavenly Father sees is quite different from the good and evil, cause and effect newsreel that we see. He sees us hidden in His love, not swamped in our circumstances.

CHAPTER 26

In The Father

Jesus was more "in His Father" than He was "in the boat" when His disciples were fearing for their lives on the Sea of Galilee. Jesus chose His own reality. Both realities pulled at Him, and He chose to rest in His Father's love rather than fear the earthly storm. And then He calmed the storm because the reality of His Father's love brings calm to the events on earth.

I was always taught that I had to pull God down into my earthly circumstances through prayer and faith. Now I understand that Jesus has set me above my earthly circumstances (I am seated in heavenly places), and my circumstances are resolved as I rest in my Father's goodness. But the resolution of my circumstances is not really the point of it all, having Jesus is the point of it all, He is actually far better than anything the earth can offer.

Sometimes we wonder where God is when we are in the midst of a storm, and we cry out to Him; we don't know how to get His attention and engage His help in our problem. But from His point of view the blood of Christ has placed us so far above our earthly strife that He might actually diminish that fact by responding as we would like…He wants us to learn to be in Him and trust His love.

The beatitude in Matthew 5:3 puts it so well. *"Blessed are the poor in spirit, for theirs is the Kingdom of God."* The poor in spirit are blessed as they lay hold of the kingdom of God, their physical need comes second; they have chosen to be rich in the love of God.

I don't mean to be uncaring or insensitive to those in need; our earthly troubles are indeed very pressing. But the scale of our earthly needs is hardly noticeable compared to the glory that will be revealed in us. We must choose which reality will fill our screen.

All that we need for life is contained in the realm of God, but we must choose to make it our home.

God knows that the thing that is best for us is that we discover how to rest in His love (which is our ultimate life). He has nothing better to offer us but that we discover His love. What is He to do when we ask Him for something that satisfies our earthly wishes at the cost of resting in His great love?

To live surrendered to the love of God is the most magnificent life possible. As we yield to it and lean back into it, the most excellent life possible begins to unfold, and we are in the middle of it. This is the movie of our lives that God planned for us.

I spent so many years thinking that God wanted me to align my will with His so that I could be His humble servant, but what a joy it has been to discover that His perfect will for me is that I live as His son, the very object of His love.

Sure, things still get done in His kingdom on the earth, but it is all the spontaneous overflow of His Spirit living in me, showing me the magnificence of my salvation, and me in turn overflowing with the sheer joy of being in Him…to a needy world.

This new movie of my life is a record of the spiritual and physical realms in seamless reality. There is no longer a dome of independence between God and me. Christ removed the separation between us, and now God's kingdom, power and glory are once again the atmosphere of my life.

Now I can see what God sees.

I can live my life from the reality that is on view before God's eyes, because it is my reality also. God has always seen me as the object of His love, even during the interval when Adam had drawn the blinds down over the unconditional love of God, He still saw me through His eyes of love. Only now I can see it too—the spiritual blindness I inherited from Adam has been healed, and I can once again see what has always been mine.

Jesus came and restored sight to the blind. Some who were physically blind had their natural eyes healed, but many more were like me and had their spiritual eyes healed so that we can live once again in His unconditional love.

Can you see it yet?

The dome of Adam's self-dependence had a ripple effect over every aspect of his life. The dome meant everything was now perceived on the basis of the physical realm, with the outcome that even the spontaneous nature of God was forced to pass through the filter of good and evil. The unconditional love of God became conditional upon our performance on the stage of human behaviour.

It must be quite perplexing for God (although I don't think He can actually be perplexed), when we present Him with our requests as if Christ had not removed the dome that separates us. God sees our full and free access to the bounty of His kingdom, yet we go to Him in prayer as if He hasn't yet decided if He will bless us.

If our prayer is not saturated in the lavish, unconditional love of God, then we are praying amiss and asking God to give us something above and beyond the extravagance expressed in the sacrifice of His Son. There is nothing more than the extravagance of Jesus' gift. Contained within it is all God has for us; it holds everything. In John 11:41, Jesus demonstrates this for us. *"Father I thank you that you have heard me."* He assumed upon the spiritual fact of His union with His Father, and Lazarus was raised from the dead as a result. But it all came from the assurance of His Father's unconditional love.

> ***Earthly provision follows a revelation of the Father's love.***

CHAPTER 27

The New Me

The Old Covenant that applied to the nation of Israel had numerous conditions governing Israel's relationship to God; some even paid with their lives for failing to measure up. But for us in the New Covenant the conditions have all been satisfied in Christ, and God fully expects that we will boldly presume upon our new status as His sons and daughters.

He wants us to assume the same rights as His Son Jesus; it is the new us.

False humility doesn't impress God. He removed the dome so that we would be exposed to His extravagance. The only thing that impresses Him is the sacrifice of Jesus—and us too, if we hide ourselves in the reality of that sacrifice.

Our true design is very unique, and it is very specific—we are joined to God through Christ. There is no alternative pathway, only Jesus; if we don't enter through Him, then we don't enter at all.

I have noticed a shift in the thinking of some Christians over the past decade. There seems to have been a merging of Christian values with Eastern spiritualism. Many value the cause of Christianity; they like its values, charity, tolerance and inclusivism. But they find it hard to locate God and so, in His place, they insert a universal divine energy. In effect they insert a philosophy in the place of a person, and Jesus is relegated to being just a good example of divine energy at work. As a result, it all comes down to where you were born and the prevailing religion of the culture in that place. It might be Buddha, Mandela, Francis of Assisi or Ghandi; each modelled his own version of how to walk in the divine energy—each produced a life worthy of admiration.

The problem with this thinking is that we land back where Adam started, presenting our lives as the measure of our individual worth.

Locating Jesus has always been difficult for Christians, because we go looking for Him among the best of human expression. Our thinking is so invested in the realm of physical activities and outcomes that we don't know how to place value on spiritual ones.

True Christianity stands apart from the herd in this regard. We do not have our focus on the best of humanity; rather, our eyes are squarely fixed on the one and only Son of God. He is the sole means whereby we stand righteously in the Father's presence. Neither we, nor any other human being who ever lived except Jesus, can convey us to stand innocently before the Most High God's holiness.

We have nothing to bring to the table—we have no inherent worth, as it were. Our worth is wholly and solely on the basis of our place as the beloved of God.

Without it we are nothing,
and with it we are everything.

Satan was the first to attempt to value himself on the basis of his personal attributes; beauty, wisdom, status—they all corrupted him as he pursued his agenda of independent authority apart from the gift of God's divine life. Adam and Eve followed suit and attempted to construct their own form of independent value out of their management of good and evil. And all of humanity that followed has also been caught up in the foolishness of self-generated worth.

But there is no life apart from the life we receive from God. Jesus spoke of it in John 5:26—*"For as the Father has life in himself, so he has granted the Son to have life in himself"*—and then later in John 10:10—*"I came that you may have life."* We have no inherent life from which to fabricate our worth unless we are joined to the Father through Jesus.

It is free and it is pure, but it cannot be blended with our own self-effort.

Jesus came to give life to the spiritually dead, not to prop up those who are doing their best.

Jesus didn't come to improve us; He came to kill us (the old self-natured man). He came to end the reign of self-made humanity and re-birth us as the Spirit-energised ones.

That may sound like heresy to some, but give it time.

John 3:19-21 adds clarification. *"This is the verdict: Light has come into the world, but men loved darkness instead of light because their deeds were evil. Everyone who does evil hates the light, and will not come into the light for fear that their deeds will be exposed. But whoever lives by the truth comes into the light, so that it may be seen plainly that what they have done has been done through God."*

Men do not actually love natural darkness; but they do love spiritual darkness, and they love the way that the dome of self hides the light of God's penetrating holiness from them. The truth of God removes the cover of our self-confidence and exposes us to a glory that transforms us into people through whom God's life flows, spontaneously expressing itself in great works of love.

I am convinced that the darkness to which this Scripture is referring is not the murky, underworld stuff like criminals hiding in shadowy doorways; it is ordinary people like you and me who have so much of ourselves invested in our self-generated worth that we cannot imagine a life entirely sustained by the righteousness of Jesus. Sure, we like the concept of salvation by grace, but we cannot imagine casting caution to the wind and depending on it to truly and deeply sustain our being—not just to give us a pleasing theological position, but to actually entrust our entire existence into its fidelity. We like the idea that God is good, but we are reluctant to kick away all of our self-made props and count on His goodness to carry us through *everything*.

This is why (over the previous pages), I clarified our desire to have God come through when we have a physical need, but we hardly ever consider the far bigger fact of our spiritual need. We have remade God into a religious teller machine that doles out solutions to our physical needs, when in reality He is our father to whom we relate because of His great love, not His ability to fix things when called upon.

We must not reduce God to our physical supplier.

I recently spoke to someone who was grappling with a great physical need and spoke of holding God accountable to His promises. Personally I don't believe we need to hold the greatest love in the universe accountable for anything; He demonstrated His commitment at the cross, and I think it is offensive that we throw religious clichés in His face.

> *In my view,*
> *we become overwhelmed by our physical circumstances*
> *because we haven't grasped the scale of God's solution*
> *to our spiritual circumstances.*

If we could see the immeasurable undertaking that He completed for us in the spiritual realm, then we would rest easy in the natural realm, knowing that a love so great will see us through, he will never leave us nor forsake us.

That is faith.

CHAPTER 28

Spirit And Truth

Our biggest problem is that we find it hard to believe in an invisible truth when we are hard-pressed by physical evidence to the contrary.

Faith is not mustering up all our reserves to stand strong against harsh opposition (that would be Adam's way). Faith is resting in the invisible fact that Jesus stood up to the opposition and that our battle is won by Him, not us.

Nor is faith an intellectual response to physical evidence where we weigh the pros and cons in the balance, and pick the most convincing option. Faith is not derived from the physical realm. It is not an intellectual process, nor is it a matter of our personal determination. It is an invisible spiritual truth which shines so brightly in our hearts that we let go of all our earthly responses and simply rest in God.

Jesus said to the woman at the well that those who worship God must do so in spirit and in truth, and the same applies to everything we do. There is no place for the fleshly motivations of Adam in the context of God's kingdom; all we do must be done in spirit and in truth. That goes for prayer, meditation and service of any kind just as much as it does for worship.

There is only one currency in the kingdom of God; it is the currency of spirit and truth, and we engage in God's economy when we rest in the efficacy of the blood sacrifice of Christ alone.

The dome of humanity's self-obsession has concealed the thing we have been trying to participate in all along. God's love and life is conveyed to us in spirit and in truth, not by the obligations of lifestyle and religion.

Jesus is Spirit, and He is truth—
and we come to God in Him.

We do not come to God in our theology of Jesus; we come to God in the person of Jesus, so we must discover how to be *in* him, not just know *about* him.

The only way we can come in Him is to step out of the identity to which we have become so accustomed, and step into our new identity as those hidden with Christ in God (Colossians 3:3). To do this, we must personally discover and embrace the outcomes of the cross of Christ. The cross of Christ changed us, it rebirthed us as sons and daughters of God, and we personally take possession of that change when we cast off the identity of Adam with all of its self-securities and insecurities and put on the freely given identity of Christ (which is already completely secure in God's love).

We no longer exist apart from our union with God. It is the new us. The old man is gone, and the new one takes over our existence. We are born of God.

There is no "spirit and truth" in Adam's alternative. God's original design of humanity is the only option that is based on spirit and truth. There is no "spirit and truth" in self-focused religion; there is only flesh and lies. God is not moved by flesh and lies.

Satan introduced Adam to a life of flesh and lies, and Jesus returned us to God's way—spirit and truth. The con that satan pulled on Adam was to convince him that his flesh was capable of procuring spiritual status through its management of good and evil; this was the ultimate lie, and it has defined human existence ever since.

The tentacles of this lie have reached into every field of human endeavour, but none with more disastrous consequences than in the church itself.

We have been urged to present God with a pleasing lifestyle to secure His favour. We have been told to mirror the life of Jesus as the perfect example of human expression. We have been told to serve the poor and hungry, the downtrodden and disenfranchised as our truest identity, to the extent that our Christianity is now more defined by our expression on the theatre of life on earth, than our existence in Christ as eternal beings made perfect by His blood. As important as these earthly activities are they pale in comparison to the life of Christ within us, that is what defines us.

We have exchanged the best for the good.

When Jesus said in John 6:63, *"The Spirit gives life, the flesh counts for nothing,"* He was saying more than that our flesh produces sin; He was saying that, without His Spirit, all that we do counts for nothing. So the exhortations to pursue Christian activities and lifestyle (as an end in itself) is worth absolutely nothing. Only Spirit-energised endeavours produce life; all the rest counts for nothing.

We have become so accustomed to the mantras of modern Christianity that they have all but drowned out the voice of the Spirit. "Be your best," "you are a champion," "be the hero inside you," are the catch cries of the age we are in, but these all flow from the thinking of Adam, not Jesus.

Jesus would say to us, "Rest in My unconditional love, and I will fill you with such life that works of love will spontaneously well up from My Spirit in you.

"You don't have to be or do anything in yourself but to discover the new 'born of God' you which I gave you on the cross.

"Trust Me; I can do more through you of lasting value in five minutes than a whole lifetime of slavish human effort will produce. I can do it, but only if you trust Me to. I can't lead you into the best version of your life if you are not ready to surrender your existence to My unconditional love. I force no one. You either embrace Me for who I am or live out a life of religious obligation. The choice is yours."

The adventure of a lifetime beckons,
but we must choose to have it.

CHAPTER 29

Life In The Spirit

As we approach the conclusion of this book, you will be aware that I am suggesting that a life in the Spirit is available to us if we will look beyond the dome of human effort and lock on to the vista of God's unconditional love.

If you have caught a glimpse of this magnificent vista, then you are part of a minority group—those who are willing to sell all to purchase the pearl of great price. Yet this minority group is steadily growing. Those who hear the Spirit's call and are drawn towards the voice of God's love are finding that others too have been captivated by it, and a strange gathering of spiritual pilgrims is forming all around the world.

There is a far-off look in their eyes. They see more than the immediate and temporal; they have looked into eternity and seen themselves there, hidden in Christ. Another world has captivated them, an unseen world where they boldly stand before God as sons and daughters of His love… they have moved on. They remain physically located on planet earth for the time being, but their true identity is beyond here. They have taken their place around the great banqueting table with the others who heard the call. They are home even before the veil of the natural realm has been drawn away.

These strangers are an unlikely gathering. They have come together from all walks of life and all levels of financial and social standing. They have become a congregation of equals made so by the blood of the Lamb.

They have one thing in common—they came to the end of themselves and escaped the cycle of Adam's inward-looking sense of security. They draw no security from their earthly status (be it great or small). They are entirely defined by the work that Christ accomplished at the cross in restoring to them the nature of God for which they were designed. Their newfound identity outshines all that the world has to offer.

Some would say they are a motley crew of misfits, but that is not so; these are the sons and daughters of the Most High God who have chosen to clothe themselves in the virtue of Christ, and in so doing have given up the compulsion to fit in down here just for the sake of impressing the masses.

> *They are comfortable in their own skin—*
> *the skin of righteousness,*
> *the skin of eternal life,*
> *and the skin of divine love—*
> *they have become truly human.*

Adam remade us to strive for our identity, but Jesus returned us to the old way of resting in the identity of God.

In some respects nothing matters anymore for this gathering. The world can't injure them anymore because they have moved on to eternity where the goodness of God is the air they breathe. Man can't hurt them and the sting of life and death on planet earth has passed; they are in the world but not of the world. Eternity has begun.

> *It has cost them everything, yet nothing.*

It costs everything because they have given up all of the props they had set up around themselves to provide for their security, identity and sense of worth; but it has cost nothing because they have freely received a new security, identity and worth from the heart of God.

They struggled with this. They knew this was more than a new theological position, that it was in fact the death of their old self and the birth of a faith that God would raise up a new self in its place. And they went ahead because they glimpsed a life hidden in the love of God; they knew it was the life for which they were born, and so they sold everything to possess this pearl of great price.

The transition from a self-based person to a God-born person is the greatest transition in human history. We do not make this journey easily because the pull of Adam's thinking holds us back. Some attempt to contain this God-born life in their theology, declaring that they agree with what I am saying. But the test is whether we can actually die to self, which is more than a theological position; it is the end of our life as we know it.

Some are active in the church, and some look for fellowship in less structured environments. In the end, it is our union with Christ that counts; and our relationship to the earthly system comes second. We don't diminish the value of fellowship and service within a local church community, but rather we elevate the value of Christ to such a lofty place that He begins to outshine everything—the good has been replaced by the best.

> **Jesus has taken over from Adam,
> and we are lost in the surpassing spectacle of His love.**

In the final analysis there are not many who come to the end of themselves. There is no stampede of people who choose to die to their old selves; most are not finished with themselves yet, so they pass up the opportunity for a future day. Jesus Himself said in Matthew 7:14, *"But small is the gate and narrow the road that leads to life, and only a few find it."* Yet if we could glimpse the scale and wonder of this life, we would abandon the old way in a heartbeat and cast ourselves into the lover of our souls.

Few find it, because they haven't come to the end of themselves.

The end of ourselves is a future beyond the dome of self-dependence. No one can convince us to step into this future because it can come only from within us as we personally take the message of the gospel and redefine our entire being according to its claims. The masses look to the gifted preacher or the mass-media teacher (and these may have their place), but in the end we must each stand alone before the cross of Christ and determine who we are as a result of it.

If the dome of our self-security dissolves as we gaze at such a love, we may dare to hide ourselves forever in it—losing all that we are that we might gain Christ.

Our old friend Truman had to believe there was more out there for him in order to venture beyond the world that was all he had ever known; I liked his style.

We, though, are not the subjects of a movie; we, unlike Truman, are not insulated in a neatly arranged set where everyone is nice to us. We are in a world that has hidden our true identity from us; we have been robbed of it. It is an identity that is completely at home in the unconditional love of God, and we need to take hold of this identity to become our true selves again.

Revelations 10:2 describes an angel who planted his right foot on the sea and his left foot on the land, and we are like that angel—we have a foot in two realms. The earth and eternity hold us; they both lay claim to us, but only one can have our true identity, only one can lay claim to us.

> *Salvation is not asking Jesus into our world,*
> *but realising that we have been accepted into His.*

Jesus has done His part—He has secured our release. Now it is up to us to stand in our new identity.

Can you see it?

Adam and Eve stood before the two trees and made their choice, and now we stand before the cross of Jesus and are offered the choice again.

Who will you be?

Cheers,

Graeme

www.ingramcontent.com/pod-product-compliance
Lightning Source LLC
Chambersburg PA
CBHW072101290426
44110CB00014B/1775